De Havil

Military 1920–64

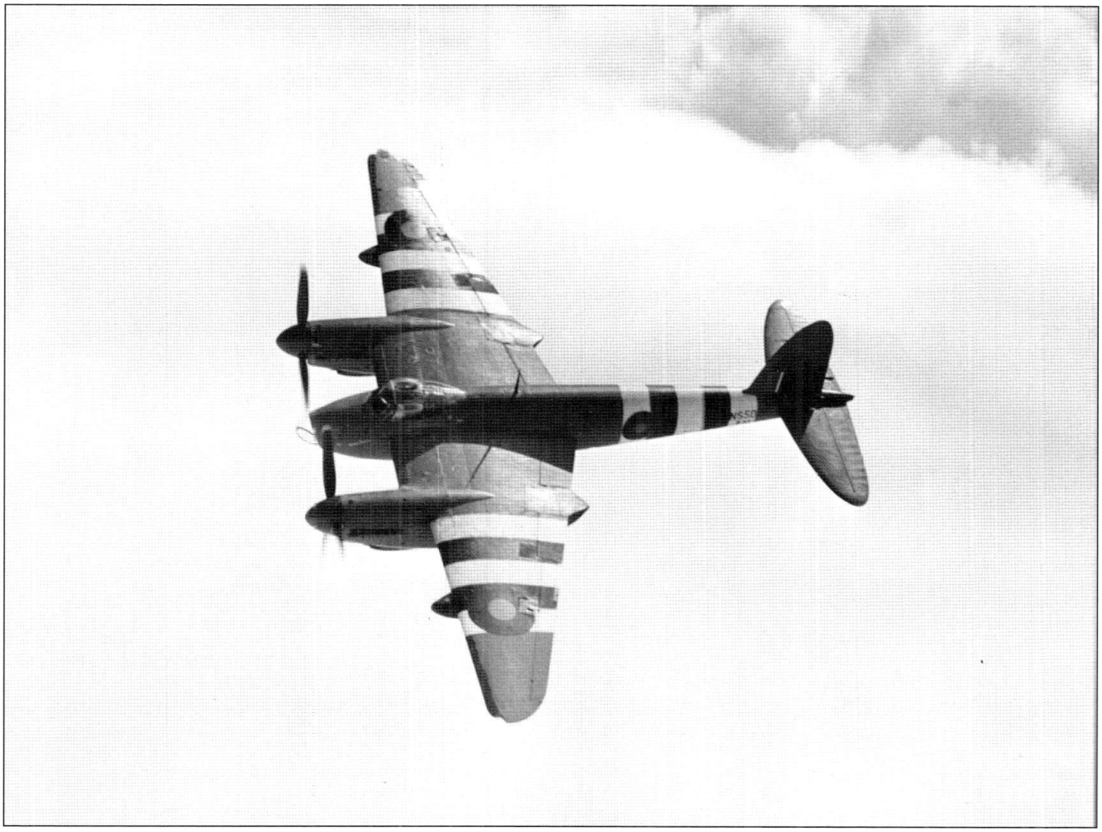

KEY Books

AVIATION INDUSTRY SERIES, VOLUME 8

Front cover image: One of the most outstanding and totally overlooked de Havilland designs ever to fly was the wonderful Hornet, a single-seat twin-engined fighter. Having entered service just a little too late to serve in World War Two, the aircraft's service career was destined to be short, and all who flew it knew how lucky they were to be in command of such a powerful fighter. (*Aeroplane*)

Contents page image: Mosquitos B.35 VP185, VP194 and TK620 line up on RAF Hemswell's Runway 06 not long after the unit made the short move from Coningsby in April 1950.

Back cover image: Comet 4 XV814 (ex-G-APDF) resplendent in the RAE's 'raspberry ripple' colour scheme.

Published by Key Books
An imprint of Key Publishing Ltd
PO Box 100
Stamford
Lincs PE9 1XQ

www.keypublishing.com

Original editions published as *Aeroplane*'s *Company Profile De Havilland (Military Types) 1920-1964* © 2014, edited by Martyn Chorlton

This edition © 2023

ISBN 978 1 80282 770 5

All rights reserved. Reproduction in whole or in part in any form whatsoever or by any means is strictly prohibited without the prior permission of the Publisher.

Typeset by SJmagic DESIGN SERVICES, India.

Contents

Introduction 4	D.H.98 Mosquito (Night Fighter) 65
The de Havilland Story 6	D.H.98 Mosquito (Photo Reconnaissance) 68
D.H.1 12	D.H.98 Mosquito (Trainers and Tugs)............. 72
D.H.2 14	D.H.98 Mosquito (Fighter Bomber) 74
D.H.3 16	D.H.98 Sea Mosquito 76
D.H.4 18	D.H.100 Vampire F.1 and 2 78
D.H.5 20	D.H.100 Vampire F.3 80
D.H.6 22	D.H.100 Sea Vampire 82
D.H.9 and 9A 24	D.H.100 Vampire FB.5 and 9 85
D.H.10 Amiens 26	D.H.100 Vampire (Export Variants) 90
D.H.11 Oxford 28	D.H.103 Hornet F Mk 1 to 4 92
D.H.29 Doncaster 30	D.H.103 Sea Hornet F Mk 20, NF Mk 21
D.H.27 Derby 32	and PR Mk 22 94
D.H.42 Dormouse and Dingo 34	D.H.104 Devon C Mk 1, 2 and
D.H.53 Humming Bird 36	Sea Devon Mk 20 98
D.H.56 Hyena... 38	D.H.106 Comet C Mk 2, T Mk 2
D.H.60 Cirrus and Genet Moth 40	and R Mk 2 100
D.H.60M Gipsy Moth 44	D.H.106 Comet C Mk 4 102
D.H.82 Tiger Moth 46	D.H.108 Swallow 104
D.H.82B Queen Bee 50	D.H.110 and Sea Vixen FAW Mk 1 108
D.H.84M Dragon 52	D.H.110 Sea Vixen FAW Mk 2........................ 110
D.H.86B 54	D.H.112 Venom FB.1 and 4.............................. 112
D.H.93 Don 56	D.H.112 Venom NF.2, 2A and 3 116
D.H.95 Flamingo 58	D.H.112 Sea Venom 118
D.H.89M and D.H.89B Dominie	D.H.113 Vampire NF.10..................................... 120
Mk I and II.. 60	D.H.115 Vampire T.11... 122
D.H.98 Mosquito (Bomber)................... 64	D.H.114 Heron and Sea Heron....................... 124

Introduction

While de Havilland Company Limited did not come into being until 1920, this book covers the period from Geoffrey de Havilland's first attempts to fly in 1909, through to his departure from Airco in 1920. This crucial, early part of de Havilland's career saw him rise from an enthusiastic amateur designing his own aircraft in a shed to a key figure and test pilot, working for the fledgling Royal Aircraft Factory at Farnborough within a relatively short space of time. By the beginning of World War One, de Havilland had become chief designer at Airco, where he created several successful military machines, including the D.H.2, D.H.4 and D.H.9A. The latter was destined to serve on into the 1930s and provide Geoffrey's own company with some vital 'bread and butter work', which helped to drag it through the first decade of its existence.

One of de Havilland's strengths was knowing when to pitch the right type of aircraft to the market at the right time, which resulted in very few military machines appearing during the 1920s and early 1930s. On the back of the Moth craze, the iconic Tiger Moth made its appearance in the mid-1930s, launching de Havilland back on to the military scene with a vengeance. While the Tiger Moth is well-known for its outstanding service as a trainer, there is only one aircraft that the majority will speak of when it comes to de Havilland and its contribution to World War Two – the Mosquito. The world's first multi-role combat aircraft, this private-venture left the competition standing when it first appeared in 1940 and continued to rule the roost right to the end of the war. Its performance and operational success was incredible, and its adaptability saw it excel in the role of a bomber, night fighter, fighter bomber, photographic reconnaissance and maritime strike aircraft.

De Havilland was quick off the mark when it came to the jet engine, and having Frank Halford as part of the team meant that the company could introduce the RAF's second jet fighter into service,

The 7,781st and last Mosquito outside the production hangar at Chester on 15 November 1950, with some of those who built it. (via *Aeroplane*)

the Vampire. De Havilland also produced its own engines, beginning with the successful Gipsy, which powered the Tiger Moth, Devon and Heron and, after buying Frank Halford's company, the Goblin and Ghost jet engines, the latter powering the early Comets, were also produced by de Havilland Engines. Other subsidiaries also included de Havilland Canada and de Havilland Australia, the former being responsible for the design of the Tiger Moth replacement, the D.H.C-1 Chipmunk.

Despite losing both of his sons in aircraft accidents, Geoffrey de Havilland remained at the helm of his company right to the end when it was eventually consumed by the Hawker Siddeley Group. His contribution to the British aircraft industry was colossal, and many of the aircraft covered in this book have remained household names from the day that they first flew. Tiger Moth, Mosquito, Vampire, Venom, Comet and Sea Vixen are just a few; all of them sewn into the tapestry of an industry that, only a few decades ago, led from the front.

The de Havilland Story

Talented designer

Along with his brothers, Ivon and Hereward, Geoffrey de Havilland was mechanically minded from a young age. After his education at Rugby and St Edward's School, Oxford, Geoffrey graduated to the Crystal Palace Engineering School, which he attended from 1900 to 1903. Whilst at the school, he built a motorcycle, complete with engine, which he used to commute to and from his home at Crux Eaton. Geoffrey's older brother Ivon, who was equally adept with mechanical engineering, became chief designer of the Iris Motor Company in Willesden. After moving to Walthamstow, Geoffrey designed one of the first buses for the Motor Omnibus Construction Company in 1906. It was while working for this company that he first met F. T. Hearle, a marine engineer from Cornwall, who was working for the Vanguard Omnibus Company as a mechanic. Hearle was destined to become Geoffrey's brother-in-law and long-serving business associate.

In the background, since being a boy, Geoffrey's attention had been distracted by the many individuals at the time who were attempting to fly in a variety of primitive machines. It was only a matter of time before Geoffrey turned his attention to aircraft and, in 1908, he borrowed £500 from his grandfather and began designing a 45hp four-cylinder water-cooled aero engine. With a power to weight ratio of less than half of the Wright Brothers' engine, Geoffrey only spent half of the budget on its manufacture, which was carried out by the Iris Motor Company, Scrubbs Lane, Willesden.

Geoffrey needed somewhere to build his aircraft and, after renting a workshop off Bothwell Street, Fulham, he set to work on his first flying machine with the help of Hearle. A wire-braced biplane, the aircraft had a front elevator, bicycle wheel undercarriage and the structure was covered in cotton, which was hand sewn by Geoffrey's wife, Louise. The completed aircraft was transported to Seven Barrows on the North Hampshire Downs in 1909 to be erected in a shed that had previously been used by J. T. C. Brabazon. Geoffrey had to wait until December for the conditions to become calm enough for the delicate aircraft to be test flown in. When the day finally came, Geoffrey took off downhill and momentarily became airborne before the wings failed and the aircraft crashed to the ground, luckily without injury to its pilot.

Sir Geoffrey de Havilland (27 July 1882–21 May 1965).

Geoffrey de Havilland Jr, with observer John E. Walker by his side, takes the prototype Mosquito E0234 into the air for the first time from Hatfield on 25 November 1940.

Not put off by his near-death experience (aviation had claimed many young lives during this pioneering period), Geoffrey set about building his second biplane. The original aircraft's spars were made of standard white wood, while this machine would employ more suitable spruce and ash. The engine was re-positioned in a pusher arrangement driving a single propeller. On 10 September 1910, Geoffrey, once again at Seven Barrows, flew the second biplane on a successful maiden flight for a distance of quarter of a mile. Not long after, Geoffrey took Hearle aloft and, the following month, his wife and eight-month-old son, Geoffrey Jr, who was destined to become his father's chief test pilot, were also flown as passengers in the second biplane.

In late 1910, the biplane was transported to Farnborough, where it was re-erected, flown by Geoffrey for a one-hour acceptance test on 14 January 1911, and then bought by the War Office for £400. The very same aircraft was used by Geoffrey to gain his Royal Aero Club Certificate (No 53) on 7 February 1911. Not long after, both Geoffrey and Hearle were employed by H. M. Balloon Factory as designer/pilot and mechanic, respectively, while the second biplane was re-designated as the F.E.1. The aircraft crashed on 15 August and Geoffrey produced a revised version, the F.E.2, powered by a 50hp Gnome rotary, which made its maiden flight just three days later. A completely different aircraft to the F.E.1, it was in this machine that Geoffrey gained his R.Ae.C. Special Certificate (No 4) by flying 100 miles to Shrewton and back from Farnborough on 6 December 1911.

Royal Aircraft Factory

The Army Aircraft Factory (ex-H. M. Balloon Factory) became the Royal Aircraft Factory in 1912 and all civilian employees were offered commissions in the Special Reserve. Geoffrey became a Second Lieutenant so that he could fly on manoeuvres also but continued in his civilian role.

With F. M. Green in assistance, Geoffrey designed the canard pusher S.E.1 in 1911 and, working closely with H. P. Folland, helped to produce the ground-breaking B.E.1 tractor biplane. He was also involved in the B.E.2, which he flew in company with Maj F. H. Sykes, to a height of 10,560ft on 12 August 1912; this was a new British attitude record. Geoffrey demonstrated the B.E.2 at the Larkhill Military Aeroplane Competition and, although the aircraft was ineligible to compete, it was far superior to the Cody design that won the event.

In March 1913, Geoffrey injured himself in the B.S.1, which spun into the ground off a turn because of poor rudder control. Redesigned and repaired, the result was the B.S.2 (later S.E.2). This was the last Royal Aircraft Factory aircraft that Geoffrey was involved in before he accepted the position of chief designer with Aircraft Manufacturing Company, Limited (more familiarly known as Airco from late 1918), owned by George Holt Thomas and based at The Hyde, Hendon, in June 1914. Two months later, World War One broke out and Geoffrey was called up for service with 2 Squadron based at Farnborough. He was destined only to serve with the unit for a few months before it was realised that his talents were better employed as a designer, and he was duly promoted to captain before continuing his work at Hendon. It was from 1915 onwards (beginning with the D.H.1) that Geoffrey's skill as a designer began to shine through and successes with the excellent D.H.4 and the later D.H.9A put the name 'de Havilland' on the aviation map.

The de Havilland Aircraft Company Limited is born

Post-war, Airco quickly found its feet in the peacetime marketplace, which gave Holt Thomas the opportunity to sell the company to the Birmingham Small Arms Company Limited (BSA) in 1920. Geoffrey had no intention of spending the rest of his career designing cars and, the same year, he left the company and formed his own, the de Havilland Aircraft Company Limited on 25 September 1920. Partly financially supported by Holt Thomas, Geoffrey became the director and chief designer and cherry-picked staff from the Airco days, including C. C. Walker (chief engineer), F. T. Hearle (general manager), W. E. Nixon (secretary), F. E. N. St Barbe (sales manager) and A. E. Hagg (assistant designer).

De Havilland's most successful interwar military type was the long-serving D.H.9A, which was used by the RAF from 1918 to 1931.

A large field was rented at Stag Lane, Edgeware, and the two wooden aircraft sheds there became the first home of Geoffrey's new company.

Wisely, the company embarked on producing civilian aircraft, although a pair of D.H.14 day bombers and a large refurbishment contract for the D.H.9As could not be sniffed at. The company achieved huge success with its civilian designs, while military types such as the D.H.27, D.H.42 and D.H.56 were found wanting. As a result, rather than waiting for poorly prepared military specifications, de Havilland began producing military machines as private ventures. The first examples were the D.H.65 Hound and the D.H.77 interceptor fighter, which appeared in 1929. Despite its best efforts, the Air Ministry was disinterested, and de Havilland continued to focus on civilian aircraft for the next ten years.

Move to Hatfield

It was only a matter of time before the Stag Lane location on the edge of London would succumb to development, and this began when the Underground system was extended to Edgeware. In 1930, a second airfield was purchased further north near Hatfield and, on 28 July 1934, Capt Geoffrey de Havilland flew out of Stag Lane for the last time in a Hornet Moth.

In the meantime, a large new factory was constructed at Hatfield, which was producing Tiger Moths, Moth Minors, Dragons and Rapides at some rate, not to mention the beautiful DH.88 Comet racers. The Albatross and Flamingo airliners followed, and sub-contract work in the shape of 1,440 Airspeed Oxfords showed that de Havilland was prepared for aircraft production on a major scale.

It was the wonderful Mosquito that dominated the company's war effort, and which saw 6,710 of these 'Wooden Wonders' built by de Havilland both at Hatfield and its new No 2 Factory at Leavesden. Various sub-contractors and the Canadian and Australian companies also contributed to a final total of 7,781, with the last of them built in 1950. The de Havilland Repair Organisation repaired 2,962 Mosquitoes, Hurricanes and Spitfires, plus a variety of de Havilland types at Hatfield and Whitney. The company's own Rolls-Royce Merlin repair department overhauled 9,022 engines.

Hatfield during the 1930s, just before expansion began to take hold.

At least 50 unidentified Mosquito FB.IVs on the Hatfield production line are visible here, being produced six abreast from the second row back.

Propeller production also became a de Havilland specialism, and this dated back to the Comet racers that were installed with variable pitch propellers. A licence to manufacture the American Hamilton propeller was acquired and, using the facilities that still remained at Stag Lane, the first of them was delivered in July 1935. Between 1939 and 1945, 102,000 propellers were made, 23,210 at Stag Lane, which had also become the Engine Division (later The de Havilland Engine Company Limited). During the same period, 10,212 Gipsy Major and Gipsy Queen engines were made at Stag Lane. More than 8,000 Tiger Moths were built in Britain and abroad, half of these by Morris Motors Limited, Cowley. Two hundred Rapides, and later Dominies, were built at Hatfield, and once production of the latter was transferred to Brush Coachworks at Loughborough, a further 275 were built. The Airspeed Company was purchased by de Havilland in 1940 and, as well as a total of 4,462 Oxfords, 695 Horsa gliders were built too.

De Havilland entered the jet era early with the Halford Goblin-powered Vampire, the prototype of which first flew on 20 September 1943, just 16 months after it was given the go ahead by the Air Ministry. The final de Havilland design to appear before the war's end was quite possibly the most attractive ever made by the company and, because it was too late for action, it is often overlooked in military history. The twin-Merlin-powered Hornet first flew on 28 July 1944, a single-seat development of the Mosquito; those who were lucky enough to fly it would never forget it.

Post-war successes and failures

De Havilland had prepared itself well for the post-war market; both civilian and military types were already in production or on the verge of entering it. The Vampire was ordered in great numbers, the little fighter being built at Chester and Preston, an ex-wartime shadow factory that was purchased by the company in 1948 and would produce 3,500 de Havilland aircraft over the following 11 years, including the Devon, Heron, Vampire and Venom. The latter, along with the Venom, would be produced as both two-seat trainer and night fighter form and would be followed by the powerful Sea Vixen all-weather fighter – the last de Havilland fighter in military service.

It was not all plain sailing for de Havilland during the post-war years. Geoffrey de Havilland suffered a personal blow when Geoffrey Jr was killed flying the D.H.108 in 1946. Geoffrey's youngest son John was also killed in a mid-air collision between two Mosquitoes in 1943. This was all too much to bear for Geoffrey's wife, Louise, who, after suffering a nervous breakdown, passed away in 1949.

Further trauma for the company as a whole came following the loss of a number Comet airliners and their subsequent grounding. But Geoffrey's 'the show must go on' attitude saw the Comet return as a much stronger and more reliable aircraft, and the knowledge gained from his son's accident in the D.H.108 helped the aviation industry as whole to understand compressibility and fatigue problems. The knowledge gained from the Comet accidents and subsequent testing was passed on to the next generation of airliner, the Trident, and the smaller, D.H.125.

From 1959, the company was owned by the Hawker Siddeley Group and, in 1964, the famous name of de Havilland disappeared for good. Sir Geoffrey de Havilland OBE, CBE, AFC, passed away on 21 May 1965, at the age of 82 at Watford Peace Memorial Hospital.

An impressive view of the main production hangar at de Havilland's Chester/Broughton factory, where 979 Vampires were built. Note integrated production of de Havilland Chipmunks.

D.H.1

Development
After joining Airco in June 1914 as chief designer, Geoffrey de Havilland's first design was the D.H.1. His influence at the Royal Aircraft Factory was sorely missed, and this machine drew heavily from the last aircraft that he had worked on at Farnborough, the F.E.2.

Design
The D.H.1 was a two-seat reconnaissance biplane with a single forward firing machine gun. The aircraft pushed very few boundaries with regard to construction, being a twin-boom layout, wire-braced, covered in fabric with twin-bay mainplanes, which were braced-internally. A pusher arrangement gave the observer/gunner an excellent field of fire and the pilot good visibility through the forward 180° but a limited view to the rear. The D.H.1 did have three original features, however, beginning with coil springs in the undercarriage, a basic oleo leg countered the rebound, and the most novel feature was a set of air brakes. The latter comprised a pair of rotatable aerofoils on either side of the fuselage to the rear of the pilot's cockpit. Approximately 3ft long, the pilot could turn them into the vertical, thus creating a form of airbrake. However, during early flights trials they were found to be ineffective and never featured on production machines. De Havilland designed the D.H.1 to be powered by the 120hp Beardmore, but this engine was in high demand for the F.E.2 and R.E.5 and the prototype and early production machines had to make do with the 70hp Renault.

Service
The prototype Airco D.H.1 was first flown by de Havilland from Hendon in January 1915. After early flight trials, a few modifications were made to the early production machines, including the fitment of more traditional rubber chord shock absorbers for the undercarriage. The observer's front cockpit had its coaming lowered to improve the pilot's visibility and to improve the rotation of the Lewis machine gun.

At least five D.H.1s were delivered to Royal Flying Corps (RFC) training units during 1915, and while planned production of the aircraft was sub-contracted to Savages, Airco focused on designing newer types. Those aircraft fitted with the intended Beardmore engine were designated as the D.H.1A and could be easily identified by the more upright six-cylinder powerplant.

Approximately 73 D.H.1s and 1As were delivered to the RFC, although only 14 Squadron in the Middle East used the six examples operationally from June 1916 until March 1917. Another 24 examples were spread across several Home Defence (HD) squadrons in Britain, and another 43 saw service with a range of training units. The type remained busy with second-line units until late 1918.

Production
A total of 100 aircraft were built, comprising 30 D.H.1s (including the prototype) and 70 D.H.1As in the serial ranges 4600 to 4649 and A1611 to A1660. Early production aircraft were built by Airco and the later production machines by Savages Ltd of King's Lynn.

Technical Data – D.H.1 and D.H.1A	
ENGINE	(1) One 70hp Renault; (1A) one 120hp Beardmore
WINGSPAN	41ft
LENGTH	(1) 28ft 11 5/8in; (1A) 28ft 11¼in
HEIGHT	(1) 11ft 4in; (1A) 11ft 2in
WING AREA	426¼sq/ft
EMPTY WEIGHT	(1) 1,356lb; (1A) 1,610lb
ALL-UP WEIGHT	(1) 2,044lb; (1A) 2,340lb
MAX SPEED	(1) 80mph; (1A) 90mph
SERVICE CEILING	(1A) 13,500ft
ARMAMENT	One .303in Lewis machine gun

The prototype D.H.1A, 4606, powered by a 120hp six-cylinder Beardmore engine, which was converted from an Airco-built D.H.1.

D.H.2

Development
During the early stages of World War One, the British were lagging behind the Germans with regard to fighter design and, in particular, its lack of a reliable interrupter gear, which allowed a machine gun to fire through a revolving propeller. As a result, de Havilland designed a smaller single-seat version of the D.H.1, which was destined to become one of the RFC's first effective fighter aircraft in combat over the Western Front.

Design
The D.H.2 looked very similar to its predecessor with the exception of a single cockpit and the fact that all of the components were slightly scaled down. An un-staggered two-bay biplane, the aircraft was fabric-covered in the traditional way, while the tail booms were constructed of tubular steel instead of wood. The tail skid was steerable, and power was provided by a 100hp Monosoupape, although a few later production machines received a 110hp Le Rhône. The single Lewis machine gun was flexibly mounted at first, but once RFC pilots mastered the technique of aiming the whole aircraft at the enemy, the weapon was fixed.

Service
The prototype D.H.2 was flown from Hendon for the first time on 1 June 1915 by Geoffrey de Havilland and, the following day, after a few adjustments, the little fighter reached 3,500ft in five minutes, which was an impressive rate of climb at the time.

24 Squadron, under the command of Maj L. G. Hawker, was the first of a dozen operational units to fly the D.H.2 from January 1916. Over the following weeks, 29 and 32 Squadron also re-equipped with the D.H.2. All three units were ready for the Battle of the Somme, where the enemy Fokkers finally met their match. Approximately 266 D.H.2s served with the British Expeditionary Force (BEF) in France and the type also equipped 5, 11, 16 and 18 Squadrons.

The D.H.2 was tremendously successfully in action, taking part in 774 combats; 24 Squadron alone claimed 44 enemy aircraft destroyed in the type. The commanding officer of 32 Squadron, Maj L. W. B. Rees, won the Victoria Cross (VC) whilst flying a D.H.2 into combat, on his own, against ten German two-seaters, shooting down a pair of them.

Only a handful saw service with HD units but one, flown by Capt R. H. M. S. Saundby, contributed to the attack that downed Zeppelin L48 at Theberton, Suffolk, on 17 June 1917. Replaced by the D.H.5 in France, the type saw additional service in the Near East with 17, 47 and 111 Squadrons, not to mention at least 100 aircraft that served with training units in Britain. The D.H.2 retained a presence until the last examples were Struck off Charge (SOC) around the Armistice.

Production
In total, 453 D.H.2s were built, all of them constructed by Airco at Hendon between 1915 and 1917.

D.H.2

Technical Data – D.H.2	
ENGINE	One 100hp Monosoupape or one 110hp Le Rhône
WINGSPAN	28ft 3in
LENGTH	25ft 2½in
HEIGHT	9ft 6½in
WING AREA	249sq/ft
EMPTY WEIGHT	(Gnome) 943lb; (Le Rhône) 1,004lb
ALL-UP WEIGHT	(production Gnome) 1,441lb; (Le Rhône) 1,547lb
MAX SPEED	(Gnome) 93mph; (Le Rhône) 92mph
SERVICE CEILING	(Gnome) 14,000ft
ENDURANCE	(Gnome) 2¾ hrs; (Le Rhône) 3 hrs
ARMAMENT	One .303in Lewis machine gun

An unusual view of a D.H.2, which shows how compact the aircraft was and how effective the fixed positioning of the single .303 Lewis machine gun would be in combat.

D.H.3

Development
A design that was in complete contrast to Geoffrey de Havilland's earlier designs, the D.H.3 was a large twin-engine day bomber, which had the capability to attack targets in Germany. Before the bomber had chance to prove itself, the project was cancelled because the War Office deemed that strategic bombing was unnecessary.

Design
A large two bay biplane, the D.H.3 did draw some design features from the Royal Aircraft Factory F.E.4, a project that de Havilland had worked on. Power was provided by a pair of 120hp Beardmore water-cooled engines, which were mounted within nacelles that were positioned between the mainplanes as pushers. These drove a pair of 9ft-diameter four-blade wooden propellers that cleared the trailing edge of the wing thanks to extension shafts. The wire-braced, Warren girder, 36ft 10in-long fuselage was very slim and constructed of spruce and plywood. The aircraft was effectively a tail dragger with a single wheel main undercarriage and tail skid, although a pair of large bumper wheels under the forward fuselage made the aircraft look like it was always sitting on its tail. The D.H.3 introduced the curved rudder, which was one of the signature design features of virtually all de Havilland designs up to the D.H.103 Hornet.

The bomber had a crew of three, a pilot positioned in front of the mainplanes and front and rear gunners, each armed with a pillar-mounted .303in Lewis machine gun.

Service
The first prototype (which was not serialled) made its maiden flight in 1916 and, even with a pair of 120hp Beardmores, the D.H.3 was a good performer. Capable of carrying a 680lb load of bombs, the D.H.3 had an eight-hour endurance, which would have been more than enough when attacking German targets. The second prototype, serialled 7744, was powered by a pair 160hp Beardmores and this factor, combined with modifications, resulted in the aircraft being re-designated as the D.H.3A. Modifications included a cut-out trailing edge, which meant that the engine extension shafts could be dispensed with, cutting down on vibration and engine wear and tear.

All looked promising for the D.H.3, until the War Office cancelled a production order for 50 aircraft. Both prototype aircraft were evaluated at Upavon with positive results, only to be returned to Hendon and relegated to the aerodrome's dump. Ironically, while both machines were being burnt on the same dump on 7 July 1917, the German Air Force's Gothas were bombing London!

Production
Two prototypes were built, the second was serialled 7744 (later applied to a 1½ Strutter), as well as an order placed by the War Office for 50 production D.H.3As, serialled A5088 to A5137. The main production order was cancelled before the first aircraft was completed.

Technical Data – D.H.3 and D.H.3A	
ENGINE	(3) Two 120hp Beardmore; (3A) two 160hp Beardmore
WINGSPAN	60ft 10in
LENGTH	36ft 10in
HEIGHT	14ft 6in
WING AREA	(3) 793sq/ft; (3A) 770sq/ft
EMPTY WEIGHT	(3) 3,980lb
ALL-UP WEIGHT	(3) 5,810lb; (3A) 5,776lb
MAX SPEED	95mph
INITIAL CLIMB RATE	550ft/min
ENDURANCE	8 hrs
RANGE	700 miles
ARMAMENT	Two .303in Lewis machine guns and up to 680lb in bombs

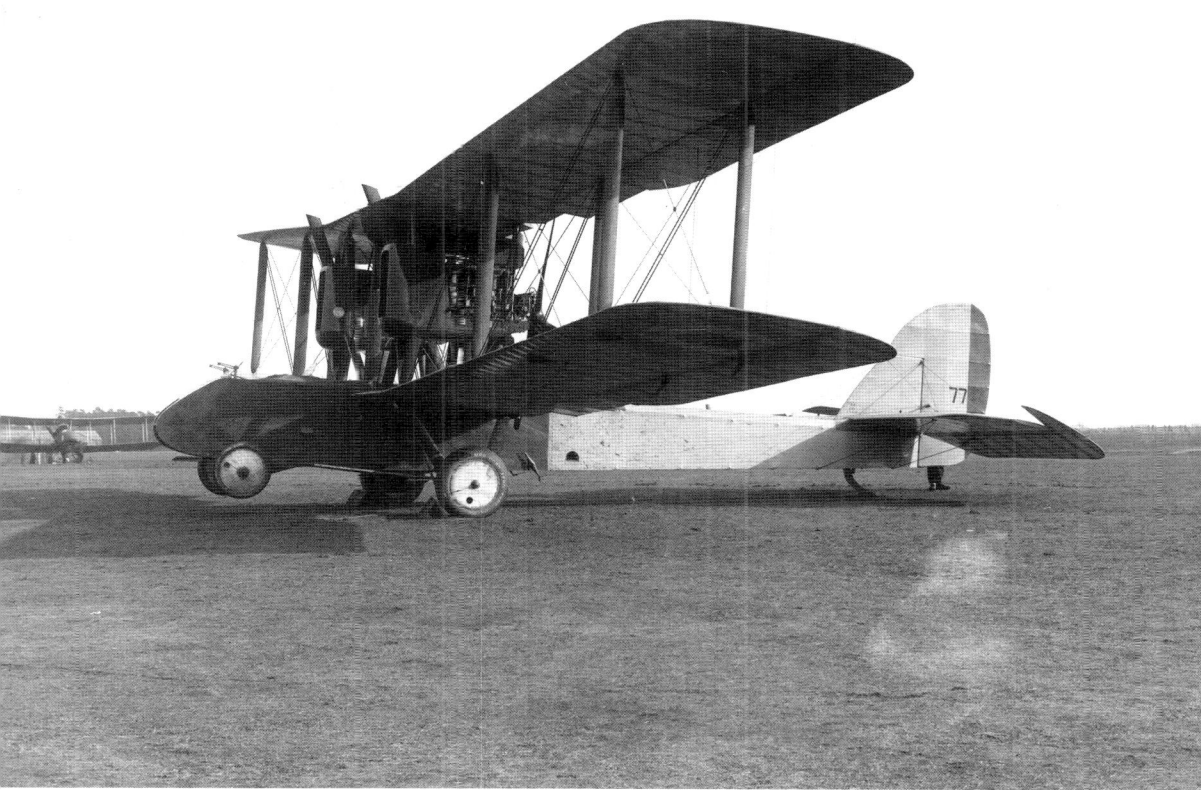

The second prototype, re-designated as the D.H.3A, serialled 7744, featured a pair of 160hp Beardmore engines, a cut-out trailing edge and direct drive four-blade propellers, rather than the extensions of the original D.H.3.

D.H.4

Development
On paper, the D.H.4 was nothing extraordinary; its original BHP engine was disappointing, and the airframe was not particularly advanced for the day. However, once the Rolls-Royce engine was made available, the aircraft was elevated to one of the most effective and well-defended day bombers of the war.

Design
A conventional design, the D.H.4 was a two-bay biplane with a wooden, fabric-covered structure, while the forward fuselage was bolstered by a layer of plywood. The tail unit was braced, and the elevator could be trimmed by the pilot, while the undercarriage was a standard fixed tail-skid design. The crew were accommodated in a pair of open cockpits, spaced apart to give the observer/gunner a good field of fire and the pilot good downward vision for bombing. This crucial separation between the two cockpits would be the type's only significant Achilles' heel.

Service
The prototype, serialled No 3696, first flew in August 1916 with a 230hp BHP (Beardmore, Halford and Pullinger), but production problems would plague this engine and it was later replaced by a Rolls-Royce unit. When fitted with the 375hp Eagle VIII, the D.H.4's performance was transformed and the type began to quickly enter service, firstly with 55 Squadron in January 1917. By April 1918, the new Royal Air Force (RAF) had nine D.H.4 squadrons while the Americans could boast 13 thanks to the mass-production of the aircraft across the pond.

Prior to its amalgamation with the RFC, the Royal Naval Air Service (RNAS) also operated the D.H.4, as did a number of HD squadrons. In the latter role, Zeppelin L.70 was brought down by a D.H.4 on 5 August 1918, crewed by Maj E. Cadbury and Capt R. Leckie. As mentioned previously, the only problem with the D.H.4 came about because of the spaced cockpits and, when under attack by an enemy fighter, communication was difficult, and many aircraft were lost because the pilot could not hear his observer/gunner's crucial instructions.

By the end of World War One, 23 RAF squadrons were equipped with the type and it was not removed from operational service until January 1919, appropriately by 55 Squadron. Post-war, the D.H.4A, which could accommodate two passengers in an enclosed cabin, also saw brief service with the RAF in small numbers.

Production
British production of the D.H.4 was 1,449 aircraft, built by Airco, Berwick, Glendower, Palladium, Vulcan, Waring and Gillow and Westland. The US aircraft manufacturers built a total of 4,846 aircraft; they were Dayton-Wright (3,106), Fisher (1,600) and Standard Aircraft (140). SABCA in Brussels also built 15 in 1926 for the Belgian Air Force.

Technical Data – D.H.4 (main data for Puma engine)	
ENGINE	One 200hp R.A.F. 3A, 230hp BHP, 230hp Siddeley Puma, 250hp Rolls-Royce Mk III or Mk IV, 260hp Fiat, 275hp Rolls-Royce Eagle VI, 300hp Renault 12Fe, 300hp Wright H, 300hp Packard 1A-1116 or IA-1237, 320hp Armstrong Siddeley Jaguar I, 325hp Rolls-Royce Eagle VII, 353hp Rolls-Royce G, 375hp Rolls-Royce Eagle VIII, Ricardo-Halford, 400hp Liberty 12, 400hp Sunbeam Matabele, 420hp Liberty V-1410, 435hp Liberty 12A, 435hp Curtiss D-12 or 525hp Packard 2A-1500
WINGSPAN	42ft 4 5/8in
LENGTH	30ft 8in
HEIGHT	10ft 1in
WING AREA	434sq/ft
EMPTY WEIGHT	2,230lb
ALL-UP WEIGHT	3,344lb
MAX SPEED	106mph
INITIAL CLIMB RATE	1,000ft/min
CEILING	17,500ft
ENDURANCE	4½ hrs
ARMAMENT	(RFC) one forward-firing .303in Vickers and one or two .303in Lewis machine guns in rear cockpit and up to 460lb of bombs

The prototype D.H.4, No 3696, pictured at Hendon around the time of its maiden flight in August 1916.

D.H.5

Development
It was only when George Constantinesco solved the problem of firing a machine gun through a revolving propeller that designers were able to redesign the scout from a pusher to a tractor configuration. This was the opportunity Geoffrey de Havilland had been waiting for to replace his own D.H.2.

Design
Known as the D.H.5, the most obvious design difference from all other de Havillands at the time was the 27in rearward stagger, which gave the pilot an excellent view upwards and forwards (but blocked the important view upwards and rearwards). The fuselage was made up of a wooden box girder, bolstered by plywood towards the front and wire-braced, making it incredibly strong. The prototype had a flat-sided fuselage with a rounded upper decking behind the engine, while the production machines were faired to a complete circular section, which tapered to an octagonal shape towards the tail. A fuel and oil tank were installed behind the pilot, and an auxiliary fuel tank was mounted above the starboard wing. A single Vickers machine gun was mounted on the top of the forward fuselage, within easy reach of the pilot, in the event of a stoppage.

Service
The prototype, serialled A5172, was first flown in August 1916 and, by December, several were in France carrying out service trials. By this time, more advanced and more heavily armed fighters were only a few months from entering service but, regardless, the D.H.5 was ordered into production.

The first recipients were 24 Squadron, based at Flez, and 32 Squadron at Léalvillers, both of which received the D.H.5 in May 1917. The D.H.5 was a pleasant aircraft to fly, but a number of early training accidents yielded unfounded rumours that the wing configuration produced a high stalling speed. In service, the aircraft was good at less than 10,000ft, but once above, performance was poor and even a Sopwith Pup could outmanoeuvre it. Heavy losses from early encounters with the enemy saw the D.H.5 withdrawn to ground attack duties, where it performed very well. The aircraft operated down low during the Battle of Ypres in August 1917 and was equipped with four 25lb Cooper bombs. 64 and 68 Squadrons excelled during the Battle of Cambrai in November. The majority of D.H.5 units were re-equipped with the S.E.5A, though 24 Squadron did not relinquish its aircraft until March 1918.

Production
There were 552 D.H.5s built, including one prototype, by Airco Ltd. (200), the Darracq Motor Engineering Co. Ltd. (200), March Jones & Cribb (100), British Caudron Co. Ltd (50) and a single machine built by No 1(Southern) ARD.

Technical Data – D.H.5 (Production)	
ENGINE	One 110hp Le Rhône or 110hp Le Clerget
WINGSPAN	25ft 8in
LENGTH	22ft
HEIGHT	9ft 1½in
WING AREA	212.1sq/ft
EMPTY WEIGHT	1,010lb
ALL-UP WEIGHT	1,492lb
MAX SPEED	109mph
INITIAL CLIMB RATE	1,200ft/min
CEILING	15,000ft
ENDURANCE	2¾ hrs

The prototype D.H.5, A5172, which first flew in August 1916.

D.H.6

Development
The demand for a primary trainer reached its peak in 1916, as the RFC began a relentless period of expansion in preparation for the decisive air battles of 1917 and 1918. The requirement was so urgent that all thoughts of aesthetics went out of the window, and the result was an aircraft that was cheap, very easy to manufacture and possibly a little too easy to fly.

Design
A very conventional biplane design, the Airco D.H.6 was mainly made of wood with a fabric covering, although a smidgeon of composite crept into the tail surfaces, which comprised steel-tube frames and wooden ribs. The undercarriage was a very rugged arrangement, complete with a tailskid and additional skids under the wingtips to protect the wings when the inevitable bad landing occurred. The whole structure was designed to be easy to maintain and repair and both upper and lower mainplanes were exactly the same, making them interchangeable. The cockpit, furnished with the most basic of instruments, was large enough for pupil pilot and instructor, who sat on the most basic of basketwork seats to eliminate any communication problems.

The only major modification the D.H.6 received during its service career was the 13½in back stagger of the mainplanes, which was later standardised into the D.H.6A.

Service
Following flight trials with the first two prototypes in 1916, serialled A5175 and A5176, the D.H.6 was found to be viceless and even un-spinnable. The stall was almost undetectable and, in an effort to prepare pupil pilots for the next stages of their flying careers, large numbers of D.H.6s were deliberately re-rigged so that they would be unstable.

Rushed into production, the D.H.6 saw widespread service with a large number of training squadrons within Britain, the Near East and at Point Cook, Australia. A number of HD squadrons had a D.H.6 on strength for communications duties but, by late 1917, the Avro 504 was taking over as the standard primary trainer. However, this was far from the end for the D.H.6, and large numbers were transferred to the RNAS for anti-submarine duties around the British coastline. Capable of carrying 100lb of bombs when crewed by just the pilot, the anti-submarine role was more of a deterrent than a concerted effort to destroy enemy submarines and, during this time, only one U-boat, UC.49, was unsuccessfully attacked in May 1918.

By the end of the war, more than 1,000 were still on RAF strength and large numbers of these were sold onto the civilian market. Examples were still flying in South Africa and Australia in the late 1930s.

Production
Approximately 2,282 D.H.6s were built by Airco, Grahame-White, Kingsbury Aviation, Harland and Wolff, Morgan and Co., Savages, Ransome, Sims and Jeffries, Gloucestershire Aircraft, Canadian Aeroplanes and Hispano-Suiza. The latter company built 60 aircraft under licence from 1921, which all served with the Spanish Air Force as primary trainers.

Technical Data – D.H.6 (R.A.F. 1A two-seater)	
ENGINE	One 90hp R.A.F. 1A, 90hp Curtiss OX-5, 80hp Renault or 140hp Hispano-Suiza
WINGSPAN	35ft 11in
LENGTH	27ft 3½in
HEIGHT	10ft 9½in
WING AREA	436¼sq/ft
EMPTY WEIGHT	1,460lb
ALL-UP WEIGHT	2,027lb
MAX SPEED	70mph
INITIAL CLIMB RATE	225ft/min
ENDURANCE	2¾ hrs

One of the two prototype de Havilland D.H.6s (either A5175 or A5176), which were produced with a traditional curved de Havilland-type rudder.

D.H.9 and 9A

Development
In response to the increasing number of air attacks on Britain from mid-1917, the Air Board decided to expand the RFC, focusing on the number of bombers it possessed. The D.H.4 was already being ordered in large numbers, but the requirement for a longer-range machine saw the arrival of the D.H.9. Not wishing to upset the already established D.H.4 production lines, de Havilland designed as much of the old aircraft into the new as possible.

Design
The D.H.9 used the same wings, tail and undercarriage as its predecessor but was given a re-designed fuselage with a streamlined nose, and the cockpits were re-positioned so that they were much closer together. The initial engine used was the 230hp BHP, but a new engine, a lightweight version called the Puma, was being developed by Siddeley-Deasy and this promised 300hp. However, development did not go well and, once the engine had been committed, it was de-rated down to 230hp and the resulting D.H.9 performed no better than the D.H.4.

To solve the power problem all eyes turned, once again, to Rolls-Royce but demand for its Eagle VIII was already exceeding supply. De Havilland was immersed in the development of the D.H.10, so it asked Westland to re-design the D.H.9 to accept the American-built Liberty engine. The fuselage was strengthened, and wings were fitted with increased span and chord to create the much-improved D.H.9A.

Service
The D.H.9 entered service with 108 Squadron in November 1917 and first went into action in northern France in March 1918 with 6 Squadron. The type's operational debut resulted in heavy losses over the Western Front, but the aircraft would prove more successful in less volatile theatres of war, such as the Middle East. It was in the latter that the D.H.9 served out its days with 55 Squadron in Egypt and Palestine until September 1920, the aircraft having already been eclipsed by the D.H.9A.

The D.H.9A began its long RAF career in June 1918 with 110 Squadron and its first taste of action came in August. Operating in tight formation at 17,000ft, the D.H.9A was a very effective bomber and, before the war had ended, it had dropped ten and half tons of bombs with very light losses. Unusually, production of the D.H.9A continued after the war and, before its retirement in 1931, the type served with 37 operational squadrons, including seven of the fledgling Auxiliary Air Force from 1925. The D.H.9A, nicknamed the 'Nine-Ack', was one of the most common post-war aircraft and was a particularly popular performer at the RAF Hendon Air Displays. Serving at home and abroad, the aircraft was ideal for policing duties over Iraq and the remote North West Frontier of India.

Production
A total of 3,200 D.H.4s were built by 16 sub-contractors (14 of them in Britain), and 1,997 D.H.9As were built between 1918 and 1927.

Technical Data – D.H.9 (Main Data for Puma Engine) and D.H.9A	
ENGINE	(D.H.9) One 230hp BHP, 230hp or 290hp Siddeley Puma, 250hp Fiat A-12, 300hp A.D.C. Nimbus, 300hp Hispano-Suiza 8Fb, 430hp Napier Lion, 435hp Liberty 12A, 465hp Wright Whirlwind R-975, 200hp Wolseley Viper, 450hp Bristol Jupiter VI or 480hp Jupiter VIII; (D.H.9A) One 375hp Rolls-Royce Eagle VIII, 400hp Liberty 12, 400hp air-cooled Liberty 12, 450hp Napier Lion or 465hp Napier Lion II
WINGSPAN	42ft 4 5/8in
LENGTH	(D.H.9) 30ft 5in; (D.H.9A) 30ft 3in; (Lion) 29ft 2in
HEIGHT	(D.H.9) 11ft 3½in; (D.H.9A) 11ft 4in
WING AREA	(D.H.9) 434sq/ft; (D.H.9A) 486¾sq/ft
EMPTY WEIGHT	(D.H.9) 2,230lb; (D.H.9A) 2,705lb
ALL-UP WEIGHT	(D.H.9) 3,325lb; (D.H.9A) 4,223lb
MAX SPEED	(D.H.9) 109.5mph; (D.H.9A) 118mph
INITIAL CLIMB RATE	(D.H.9) 625ft/min; (D.H.9A) 850ft/min
ENDURANCE	(D.H.9) 4½ hrs; (D.H.9A) 3½hrs

39 Squadron D.H.9As over Lahore during their long tour of duty in India as part of the British presence along the North West Frontier.

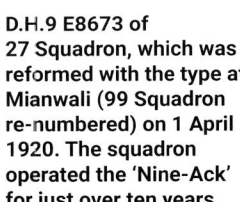

D.H.9 E8673 of 27 Squadron, which was reformed with the type at Mianwali (99 Squadron re-numbered) on 1 April 1920. The squadron operated the 'Nine-Ack' for just over ten years.

D.H.10 Amiens

Development
Rubbing shoulders with the Vickers Vimy and Handley Page V/1500 as one of the most promising late World War One bombers, the D.H.10 only saw brief service at the very end of the conflict. Destined to become the backbone of the new RAF Independent Force, the D.H.10 would have been a most effective bomber, especially for raids into Germany.

Design
Designed by Geoffrey de Havilland to Specification A.2.b for a single- or twin-engine day bomber, the D.H.10 was a direct development of the D.H.3. The first prototype was fitted with a pair of 230hp BHP engines in a pusher configuration. When evaluated, performance was found to be 6 per cent lower than the original estimate and, to rectify this, more powerful 360hp Rolls-Royce Eagle VIII engines were installed in a tractor layout. These engines transformed the performance to above expectations; the D.H.10 was faster than the D.H.9A and able to carry twice the bomb load.

The first two prototypes were officially designated as the Amiens Mk I, the third as the Mk II and the fourth, along with all production aircraft, was designated as the Mk III. The latter was powered by the 395hp Liberty 12 engine and was the most prolific example built. The Amiens Mk IIIA (aka the D.H.10A) differed in having its engines attached to the lower mainplane. The final variant, the Mk IIIC, had a few examples fitted with Eagle engines in case a shortage of Liberty engines should occur; this aircraft was designated as the Amiens Mk IIIC (aka the D.H.10C).

Service
The first prototype Amiens Mk I, C4283, made its maiden flight on 4 March 1918, followed by the third prototype, the first Mk II, C8659, on 12 April 1918. The type entered service with 104 Squadron at Azelot, northern France, in early November 1918. A single aircraft, F1867, flown by Capt E. Garland, carried out the type's one and only offensive operation of World War One on 10 November, when the bomber attacked the enemy aerodrome at Sarrebourg.

Post-war, the Amiens saw service with 216 Squadron in Egypt until June 1922, when it was replaced by the Vimy. 120 Squadron flew a mail service between Hawkinge and Cologne in 1919, with one of its D.H.10s became the first 'service' aircraft to fly mail at night on 14/15 May. The Cairo to Baghdad mail service was pioneered by a D.H.10 on 23 June 1921. D.H.10s saw action again with 60 Squadron in India during the Third Anglo-Afghan War in 1920 and 1922. The D.H.10 also saw service with 24, 27, 51, 97 and 120 Squadrons.

Production
In total, 258 Amiens were built, made up of two Mk Is, one Mk II, 221 Mk IIIs, 32 Mk IIIAs and five Mk IIICs (Mk I was later modified to Mk IIIC standard), out of an original order of 1,300 placed by the Air Ministry. The D.H.10 was manufactured by Airco, the Birmingham Carriage Company, Siddeley-Deasy, Daimler, Alliance, Mann, Egerton and the National Aircraft Factory No 2 at Heaton Chapel.

D.H.10 Amiens

Technical Data – D.H.10 Amiens Mk I, II, III and IIIA	
ENGINE	(I) two 230hp BHP; (II) two 360hp Rolls-Royce Eagle VIII; (III and IIIA) two 400hp Liberty 12; (IIIC) two 375hp Eagle VIII
WINGSPAN	(I and II) 62ft 9in; (III and IIIA) 65ft 6in
LENGTH	(I and II) 38ft 10in; (III and IIIA) 39ft 7½in
HEIGHT	14ft 6in
WING AREA	(I) 789¾sq/ft; (II) 834sq/ft; (III and IIIA) 837½sq/ft
EMPTY WEIGHT	(I) 5,004lb; (III) 5,585lb; (IIIA) 5,750lb
ALL-UP WEIGHT	(I) 6,950lb; (II) 8,050lb; (III and IIIA) 9,000lb
MAX SPEED	(I) 109mph; (II) 117½mph; (IIIA) 129mph
CLIMB to 6,500ft	(I) 11min 25sec; (III) 9min; (IIIA) 7min
SERVICE CEILING	(I) 15,000ft; (III) 16,500ft; (IIIA) 17,500ft
ENDURANCE	(I) 3½ hrs & (III and IIIA) 5¾ hrs
ARMAMENT	One of two .303in Lewis machine guns and up to 920lb of bombs

Right: The third prototype D.H.10 was the Rolls-Royce Eagle-powered C8659, which first flew on 20 April 1918.

Below: Formed as a bomber squadron with the Handley Page O/100 and O/400 in January 1918, 216 Squadron received the D.H.10 at Abu Sueir in August 1920. E5450 is pictured at Heliopolis, Egypt, in 1921.

D.H.11 Oxford

Development
A replacement for the D.H.10 in the role of a long-distance bomber, the D.H.11 Oxford only reached the prototype stage, as the entire project 'literally' stalled because of problems with the ABC Dragonfly engines.

Design
The D.H.11 had the same twin-engined, three-bay layout as its predecessor and also featured a similar fabric-covered structure, made up of wooden airframes mixed with steel tubing for the more stressed components. The latter included the engine bearers, empennage trailing edges and the undercarriage. Horn-balance rudders and the increasingly familiar de Havilland rudder were also installed.

The mainplanes gave the impression of diverging because the lower had a dihedral of two degrees and the upper four degrees. The fuselage was 6ft deep and 4ft wide, which created a substantial gap created between the mainplanes. The fuselage design allowed for a mid-upper air gunner's position, standing on a raised platform, which gave him a superb field of fire. The fuselage was spacious enough for the main fuel tanks, with a 170-gallon capacity, to be hung from the upper longerons. This gave enough room underneath for a walkway, giving access from the rear gunner's position to the cockpit and then forward to the front gunner's position. Both gunners' positions had a Scarff ring-mounted .303in Lewis machine gun, and four standard 230lb bombs could be carried internally. The radial Dragonfly engines were mounted in nacelles fixed to the lower mainplane, while the undercarriage looked like a larger version of the design fitted to a D.H.9A.

When doubts about the availability of the Dragonfly engines crept in, a version of the Oxford was designed to accommodate a pair of Siddeley Puma inline, high-compression engines. On paper, the Dragonfly-powered variant was the Oxford Mk I and the Puma-powered the Oxford Mk II (H5892). A third variant, the D.H.12 (H5893), was proposed, also powered by Dragonfly engines and with modified gunners' positions.

Service
A contract for three aircraft was placed in 1918; the fuselage of the first, serialled H5891, was nearing completion in the Hendon factory by August of that year. However, work came to a grinding halt in September because of production problems with the Dragonfly engines, and this was when the contingency plan of the Oxford Mk II was drawn up. The aircraft was completed in March 1919 and, even though the Dragonfly engines were an unproven unknown quantity, de Havilland still decided to install them. The aircraft carried out its maiden flight not long after the engines were installed, but both Dragonflies proved to be very unreliable. The engines were later re-positioned but this made little difference to reliability. The final flight took place when a connecting rod broke, causing one of the engines to seize up, but test pilot F. T. Courtney carried out an excellent forced landing without further damage. Before the year was over, the remaining two prototypes were cancelled, giving de Havilland the opportunity to put the D.H.11 Oxford behind it.

Technical Data – D.H.11

ENGINE	(I) two 320hp ABC Dragonfly; (II) two 290hp Siddeley Puma high compression
WINGSPAN	60ft
LENGTH	45ft 2¾in
HEIGHT	13ft 6in
WING AREA	719sq/ft
EMPTY WEIGHT	3,795lb
ALL-UP WEIGHT	7,027lb
MAX SPEED	117mph at 6,500ft
CLIMB to 10,000ft	13½ min
ENDURANCE	3¼ hrs
ARMAMENT	Two .303in Scarff ring-mounted Lewis machine guns and up to 1,000lb of bombs carried internally

The sole prototype D.H.11 Oxford, serialled H5891, during one its rare outings from Hendon in 1919.

D.H.29 Doncaster

Development
Although they were presented by de Havilland's as potential armed troop-carrying transports or ten-seat commercial airliners, the D.H.29 was ordered by the Air Ministry as long-range experimental monoplanes. Both aircraft were very important from a development of the British transport monoplane point of view because they were the first to be fitted with a thick section, high-lift, cantilever wing, which was initially developed for the D.H.26 project.

Design
Extensive wind tunnel testing was carried out at the old Airco works at Hendon until the facility was sold to the University of Adelaide in 1921. The D.H.29 had a crew of two positioned in an open cockpit high on the fuselage in front of the leading edge. Below them was a 345cu/ft cabin with continuous glazed, sliding windows. The main structure was spruce longerons and composite cross-struts bolstered with a plywood covering, which kept the cabin free of unsightly bracing. To give strength to the undercarriage attachment points, the floor of the fuselage was wider than the roof.

The cantilever wing, which weighed 1,050lb, was all-wood construction with internal bracing, fabric-covering with differential ailerons designed by A. E. Hagg. The wing housed the main 115-gallon capacity fuel tanks in the leading edges, feeding fuel to the engine by gravity.

Service
The first of two aircraft, serialled J6849, made its maiden flight from Stag Lane on 5 July 1921. Because the engine thrust line matched the centreline of the fuselage, flying the D.H.29 on these early flights was very uncomfortable for the pilot, who was exposed to the full force of the slipstream. Direction control was also poor and, to resolve this, the nose was re-designed, and the Lion engine was raised by 20in. This caused fuel flow problems and a header tank had to be installed with wind driven pumps. Delivered to Martlesham Heath in January 1922, J6849 also had its cabin windows modified to three smaller porthole-types. Once further modified with a dorsal gunner's cockpit, the aircraft was only then known as the Doncaster.

The second aircraft first flew in August 1921 and, despite being allocated the military serial J6850, this D.H.29 was presented as a ten-seat commercial airliner. Despite commercial interest, especially from Daimler Hire Ltd, in the aircraft, which was re-registered G-EAYO, the D.H.29 never saw airliner service.

Both aircraft made valuable contributions to the understanding of the thick-section cantilever wing, thanks to an intensive flying programme and subsequent static component testing, after they were grounded in 1924.

Production
Two aircraft were built to Specification D of R Type 4B (later 10/20) order to contract numbers 107614/21, 378100/21 and AM378100, dated 7 March 1921.

Technical Data – D.H.29 Doncaster	
ENGINE	One 450hp Napier Lion IB
WINGSPAN	54ft
LENGTH	43ft
HEIGHT	16ft 6in
WING AREA	440sq/ft
EMPTY WEIGHT	4,200 to 4,370lb
ALL-UP WEIGHT	7,273 to 7,500lb
MILITARY LOAD	1,431lb
TOTAL LOAD	2,903lb
MAX SPEED	116mph at 10,000ft
ARMAMENT	One .303in Lewis machine gun

The first of two D.H.29s built, J6849 is in its final configuration, complete with round porthole cabin windows and rear/dorsal gunner's position, at Martlesham Heath in the autumn of 1923.

D.H.27 Derby

Development
Produced to Specification 2/20, which called for an 'interim' single-engined heavy bomber, the D.H.27 Derby was the first military aircraft to be designed and built by the new de Havilland Company Limited. Only Avro punted at the same specification, with its Aldershot; both companies knew that the Air Ministry was not entirely sure about what it needed and expectations for a large contract to the winner were not high. In the end, the Aldershot proved to be the better aircraft but, regardless, only 15 production aircraft were ordered to serve with a single squadron for just 16 months before the type was replaced by the Handley Page Hyderabad when Air Ministry policy changed to the requirement for a twin-engined bomber.

Design
The D.H.27 Derby was a large twin-bay biplane constructed of all-wood with wire bracing and covered in fabric. The aircraft had many features that would be employed in the construction of de Havilland commercial types, including a variable incidence tailplane, rubber-shocked undercarriage legs with oleo dampers and a plywood covered fuselage. The undercarriage was widely spaced to give sufficient room for the carriage of a single 1,000lb, two 550lb, or four 220lb bombs below the fuselage and the 64ft 6in-span wings could be folded.

The Derby was devoid of centre section struts; instead, a large single cabane took the weight of the upper mainplane and also served as the location for the main 212-gallon fuel tank. The central fuselage served as a cabin, complete with large porthole windows on either side, as a comfortable 'office' for the navigator/bomb aimer. The pilot operated from an open cockpit ahead of the mainplanes directly behind the engine while a rear gunner, with a Scarff ring-mounted Lewis machine gun, was far back above the rear fuselage.

Service
The first of two prototypes ordered by the Air Ministry, serialled J6894, first flew on 13 October 1922, followed by the second aircraft, J6895, on 22 March 1923. Despite being fitted with the same Condor engine as the Aldershot, the Derby was much heavier than its competitor and, as a result, its performance suffered. Not being able to carry its bomb load internally was another negative against the Derby.

Following the comparative trials, J6894 was retained at Martlesham heath until March 1923 but, by May, was delivered to Grain for loading trials before moving to the Royal Aircraft Establishment (RAE) at Farnborough where it was broken up for spares. J6895 had a less useful career, the aircraft was stored at Northolt from May 1923 until January 1924 from where it was moved to Kenley and struck off in March.

Production
Two aircraft were ordered to Contract No 331693/20 dated 23 May 1921, with serials J6894 and J6895.

Technical Data – D.H.27 Derby	
ENGINE	One 650hp Rolls-Royce Condor III
WINGSPAN	64ft 6in; (folded) 30ft
LENGTH	47ft 4in
HEIGHT	16ft 10in
WING AREA	1,120sq/ft
EMPTY WEIGHT	6,737lb
ALL-UP WEIGHT	11,545lb
MILITARY LOAD	2,528lb
TOTAL LOAD	4,808lb
MAX SPEED	105mph
ARMAMENT	One Scarff ring-mounted .303in Lewis machine gun and up to 2,200lb of bombs

The first D.H.27 Derby pictured at Martlesham Heath in late October 1922, before the aircraft was evaluated against the Avro Aldershot.

D.H.42 Dormouse and Dingo

Development
In 1922, the Air Ministry issued Specification 22/22, calling for a two-seat fight/reconnaissance aircraft powered by a supercharged engine. In response, de Havilland designed the D.H.42 Dormouse. This was, in effect, the beginning of the long hunt for a Bristol F.2B Fighter replacement and only the same manufacturer would come close with its Type 84 Bloodhound, until the specification was revised. Two years later, Specification 8/24 was also issued for an Army Co-operation aircraft, de Havilland offering a more powerful version of the Dormouse in the shape of the Dingo. Neither aircraft were successful.

Design
The D.H.42 Dormouse was a traditional de Havilland-designed unequal-span biplane. Made of wood and covered in fabric, the aircraft had tandem open cockpits for the two crew. The Dormouse had a fixed tail-skid undercarriage and the fuel for its Armstrong Siddeley Jaguar engine was carried in a pair of streamlined tanks mounted on top of the upper mainplane.

The Army Co-operation D.H.42A Dingo I only differed in its powerplant, which was the more powerful 410hp Bristol Jupiter radial. The Jupiter was a larger diameter engine than the Jaguar, which meant that the two forward-firing machine guns were re-positioned from within the forward fuselage to on top of it. The third aircraft built was the D.H.42B Dingo II, which was fitted with a 435hp Jupiter. The fuselage of the Dingo II was made of steel tube and also featured bigger fuel tanks and a message pick-up below the fuselage.

Service
The D.H.42 Dormouse, serialled J7005, was first flown from Stag Lane on 25 July 1923, and, from November, made the first of several visits to Martlesham Heath for trials. J7005 was on display in the New Type's Park at Hendon on 28 June 1924, displaying '4', and later in the year was re-engined with a 420hp Jaguar IV engine. After a spell with the RAE, the aircraft made its last flight on 4 January 1926.

The D.H.42A Dingo I, J7006, made its maiden flight on 12 March 1924, and, after trials with the Aeroplane & Armament Experimental Establishment (A&AEE) and 41 Squadron, the aircraft broke up over Northolt on 5 June 1924. The D.H.42B Dingo II, J7007, was first flown by Hubert Broad on 29 September 1926. The aircraft had a short flying career with the A&AEE and, finally, the RAE; the Dingo II appears not to have flown beyond November 1926.

Production
Three aircraft were built to Contract No 391318/22 dated 17 May 1923, comprising one D.H.42 Dormouse (J7005), one D.H.42A Dingo I (J7006) and one D.H.42B Dingo II (J7007).

Technical Data – D.H.42 Dormouse, DH.42A Dingo I and DH.42B Dingo II	
ENGINE	(42) One 350hp Armstrong Siddeley Jaguar II or 420hp Jaguar IV; (42A) one 410hp Bristol Jupiter III; (42B) one 436hp Jupiter IV
WINGSPAN	(42) 41ft; (42A and B) 41ft 6in
LENGTH	(42) 39ft 6in; (42A amd B) 39ft 11½in
WING AREA	(42) 389sq/ft; (42A and B) 398sq/ft
EMPTY WEIGHT	(42) 2,513lb; (42A) 2,346lb; (42B) 2,780lb
ALL-UP WEIGHT	(42) 3,897lb; (42A) 3,700lb; (42B) 4,038lb
MILITARY LOAD	(42) 434lb; (42B) 628lb
TOTAL LOAD	(42) 1,322lb; (42B) 1,685lb
MAX SPEED	(42 with Jaguar IV) 125mph at 15,700ft; (42A) 127mph; (42B) 128mph
CEILING	(42 with Jaguar IV) 16,000ft; (42A) 17,500ft
ARMAMENT	Two forward firing .303in machine guns and one Scarff ring-mounted .303in machine gun in rear cockpit

The Dormouse had several unusual features, including the position of the pilot under the upper mainplane, with an aperture directly above. The aircraft's two streamlined saddle tanks can be seen above the upper mainplane.

D.H.53 Humming Bird

Development
During the austere post-war years, the age of the ultralight type aircraft was born, encouraged by events such as the *Daily Mail* Trials held at Lympne in 1923, 1924 and 1926. De Havilland's contribution to the first event held in October 1923 was a pair of D.H.53s named *Humming Bird* and *Sylvia II*.

Design
The first two D.H.53s built were low-wing, single-seat monoplanes powered by a 750cc Douglas motorcycle engine. The engines gave much trouble during the competition and no prizes were won, but Maj H. Hemming proved the practicality of the type by flying for 59.3 miles on a single gallon of fuel.

The Douglas engine was replaced by the more reliable 26hp (698cc) Blackbourne Tomtit two-cylinder vee piston engine. It was then that the Air Ministry began to show an interest in the little machine.

Service
The RAF ordered six aircraft for communications duties and flying practice, all of which made their public debut at the RAF Air Display at Hendon on 27 June 1925. During the event, a race between the six diminutive aircraft was held between the Air Ministry Directorates; the entertaining five-mile-long race was won by Air Cdre C. H. Longcroft.

Two more aircraft, J7325 and J7326, were ordered in 1924, both of which were specially modified with airship pick-up gear. Both aircraft would carry out experiments with the airship R33 in the art of launching and recovering a 'parasite aircraft'. The trials were carried out at Pulham and, on 15 October 1925, with J7325 hanging below the giant airship from a trapeze, the first attempt was made. At 3,800ft, Sqn Ldr R. de Haga Haig climbed down into the cockpit via a ladder; the aircraft was swung down on the trapeze and successfully launched. After diving until the engine fired, Haga Haig carried out a couple of loops before

re-engaging with the airship's hook. The exercise was successfully repeated again on 4 December in J7325 but was destined never to be repeated and the idea faded away along with the future of the airship.

All eight D.H.53s were SOC in 1927, six of them being granted Certificates of Airworthiness so that they could serve on with civilian owners.

Production

Eight D.H.83 Humming Birds were supplied to the RAF in two batches, the first for six aircraft built to Contract No 389319/22 dated 12 July 1923 and serialled J7268 to J7273. The second batch of two aircraft was to Contract No 487253/24 and serialled J7325 and J7326.

Technical Data – D.H.53 Humming Bird	
ENGINE	One 750cc Douglas, 698cc (26hp) Blackbourne Tomtit, 32hp Bristol Cherub II, 35 hp ABC Scorpion or 40hp Aeronca
WINGSPAN	30ft 1in
LENGTH	19ft 8in
HEIGHT	7ft 3in
WING AREA	125 sq/ft
EMPTY WEIGHT	(Douglas and Tomtit) 326lb
ALL-UP WEIGHT	(Douglas and Tomtit) 524 and 565lb
MAX SPEED	73mph
INITIAL CLIMB RATE	225ft/min
RANGE	150 miles
CEILING	15,000ft

The last of just eight D.H.53 Humming Birds, which briefly served with the RAF during the mid-1920s, was J7326, pictured at the Aeroplane & Armament Experimental Establishment (A&AEE), Martlesham Heath. Re-registered as G-EBQP, the aircraft stalled and crashed at Hamble on 21 July 1934.

D.H.56 Hyena

Development
A development of the D.H.42B Dingo II, the D.H.56 Hyena was another attempt to gain a military contract on the back of an Army Co-operation specification; this time it was 30/24 calling for a two-seat reconnaissance machine. The D.H.56 also found itself in company with aircraft competing for Specification 20/25 for an F.2B and D.H.9A replacement and, by the time the aircraft flew, it was up against the Short Chamois, Vickers Vespa, Bristol Boarhound and the Armstrong Whitworth Atlas.

Design
Very similar to the Dingo, the Hyena featured the de Havilland rudder, ball bearing controls, differential ailerons and a rubber-in-compression undercarriage. The 385hp Jaguar III, two-row, air-cooled radial driving a two-blade wooden propeller provided the power for the unequal span biplane. The drag-inducing wing fuel tanks of the Dingo were replaced by a main 100-gallon fuel tank fitted into the fuselage in front of the pilot. The fuel was lifted to a centre section gravity tank with a wind driven pump, which could be overridden by a hand pump in the event of an emergency.

Below the rear gunner's cockpit was mounted the message pick-up gear and the aircraft was well equipped for artillery spotting, ground attack, bombing, photographic reconnaissance and supply dropping duties; all of which were essential components of the detailed specification.

Service
The first of just two Hyenas to be built, J7780 made its maiden flight in the hands of Hubert Broad on 17 May 1925. The aircraft was first evaluated by the A&AEE in November and made its first public appearance in the New Type's Park at Hendon on 3 July 1926. Embarrassingly for de Havilland, the engine failed during the display, and it was later re-engined with the 422hp Jaguar IV. In this configuration, the aircraft was presented for testing for Specification 20/25, which included a service trial with 4 (AC) Squadron during July and August 1926. By this time, the second Hyena, J7781, had made its first flight on 29 June 1926. It joined J7780 for service trials with 4 Squadron and, later, 2 (AC) Squadron. The competition was ultimately won by the Atlas, which gave ten years' good service to the RAF.

J7780's flying career came to end in late 1926, while J7781 found further work participating in field exercises and was later transferred to the RAE Engine Flight at Farnborough in July 1927. The aircraft proved to be a useful testbed for a number of engine modification trials until it was grounded in May 1928.

Production
Two D.H.56 Hyenas were ordered to Contract No 593919/25, serialled J7780 and J7781, built to Specification 30/24.

Technical Data – D.H.56 Hyena	
ENGINE	One 385hp Armstrong Siddeley Jaguar III or 422hp Jaguar IV
WINGSPAN	(upper) 43ft; (lower) 41ft 5¼in
LENGTH	(Jaguar III) 29ft 11in; (Jaguar IV) 29ft 9in
HEIGHT	10ft 9in
WING AREA	421¼sq/ft
EMPTY WEIGHT	(Jaguar III) 2,247lb; (Jaguar IV) 2,399lb
ALL-UP WEIGHT	(Jaguar III) 3,962lb; (Jaguar IV) 4,200lb
MAX SPEED	130mph
CLIMB RATE	10,000ft in 13min 24sec
CEILING	19,230ft
ARMAMENT	One forward-firing .303in Vickers and one .303in Lewis in rear cockpit and four light bombs carried under port lower mainplane

The first of two D.H.56s built, J7780 is at Martlesham Heath on 31 July 1926, just before the aircraft was sent to Farnborough for service trials with 4 Squadron.

D.H.60 Cirrus and Genet Moth

Development
The first of many Moth-related machines to serve with the RAF was tentatively accepted into service in the late 1920s. It was not ordered in large numbers and the aircraft was not fully appreciated by the RAF, as it did not fit into the training requirements of the day. However, those that did serve were always displayed in a most spirited and enthusiastic way.

Design
The Cirrus Moth closely resembled the original D.H.60 and the RAF ordered two versions; one powered by the 60hp Cirrus I and the other by the 85hp Cirrus II air-cooled four-cylinder inline engine. The single-seat Genet Moth was also a variant of the standard D.H.60 Moth but was powered by a 75hp Armstrong Siddeley Genet I five-cylinder radial engine.

Service
The first D.H.60 Cirrus Moth, J8030, fitted with the 60hp Cirrus I, made its first flight on 13 March 1926. By the end of April, the aircraft had been allocated to the A&AEE for trials, while the two remaining aircraft from the first batch, J8031 and J8032, were sent to the Central Flying School (CFS). The first of the Cirrus II-powered machines were taken on charge in December 1927. This batch of 19 aircraft was spread thinly across the RAF, serving only in small numbers with the CFS, Electrical and Wireless School (E&WS), Andover Communications Flight (CF) and 24 Squadron, the latter between May 1928 and 1930.

Despite only six ever entering RAF service, the Genet Moth made more of a name for itself. The first aircraft, J8816, was delivered to the A&AEE in September 1925 and the remaining five production machines were taken on charge in June 1927; all six aircraft were allocated to the CFS. The following month, the six aircraft appeared at the RAF Hendon Display, where J8820, flown by Sqn Ldr Smart, carried out an excellent exhibition of crazy flying. The rest of the Genet Moths performed a variety of aerobatics with experienced CFS instructors, including four who would join the Schneider Trophy team; Flt Lt d'Arcy Greig DFC, Plt Off G. H. Stainforth, Plt Off R. L. R. Atcherley and Plt Off H. R. D. Waghorn. One aircraft, J8817, served with 4 Squadron from June 1928 to June 1929 and, in 1930, five of the batch were SOC; J8820 remained on the strength of the HAD Flight until July 1931.

Production
Three D.H.60 Cirrus Moths (60hp Cirrus I) were ordered, one to Contract 635519/25 and two to Contract 667490/26, all delivered in April 1926 and serialled J8030 to J8032. There were 19 D.H.60 Cirrus Moths ordered on Contract 806527/27 and delivered in December 1927 and into 1928, serialled J9103 to J9121. Six D.H.60 Genet Moths were ordered on Contract No 761499/27 and delivered in September 1925 (J8816) and June 1927 (J8817 to J8821).

Technical Data – D.H.60 Cirrus and Genet Moth	
ENGINE	(CM) One 60hp ADC Cirrus I or 85hp Cirrus II; (GM) One 75hp Armstrong Siddeley Genet I
WINGSPAN	(CM) 29ft; (GM) 30ft
LENGTH	(CM) 23ft 6in; (GM) 24ft 3 3/8in
HEIGHT	(CM) 8ft 7in; (GM) 8ft 9½in
WING AREA	(CM) 225sq/ft; (GM) 243sq/ft
EMPTY WEIGHT	(CM) 764lb; (GM) 810lb
ALL-UP WEIGHT	(CM) 1,240lb; (GM) 1,350lb
MAX SPEED	(CM) 91mph; (GM) 95mph
INITIAL CLIMB	(CM) 430ft/min; (GM) 360ft/min
CEILING	(CM) 13,000ft; (GM) 12,500ft
RANGE	(CM) 320 miles; (GM) 290 miles

Allocated to 24 (Communications) Squadron at Northolt in June 1928, J9104 was later wrecked and caught fire after a heavy landing at the station on 4 September.

J8820 being put through its paces; the aircraft was wrecked at Wittering when it stalled inverted and crashed on 13 June 1930. The aircraft was transferred to the Home Aircraft Depot Flight in July 1931.

The first D.H.60 Cirrus Moth was J8030, which first flew on 13 March 1926, and was taken on charge by the RAF on 28 April at the A&AEE, Martlesham Heath.

D.H.60M Gipsy Moth

Development
The D.H.60 Gipsy Moth was already a common sight across the country in civilian hands by the time it was taken on strength by the RAF as an ab initio trainer and communications aircraft. The first Moth, powered by a 60hp Cirrus engine, was G-EBKT, which made its maiden flight on 22 February 1925. The aircraft was a huge success for de Havilland from the start and was instrumental in establishing a large number of new flying clubs across the country.

Design
The very first Gipsy Moth appeared in 1928 was designated as the D.H.60G. The aircraft was a development of the original D.H.60 but was powered by a 100hp Gipsy engine, instead of a Cirrus unit. The early aircraft were all-wood construction but, in 1929, a metal version was built, designated the D.H.60M, and it was this variant that was ordered by the RAF. The aircraft met the requirements of Specification 4/29 for an ab initio trainer and an order for 135 was placed.

Service
The Gipsy Moth entered RAF service with 5 Flight Training School (FTS) at Sealand and was quickly followed by 3 FTS at Spittlegate, the RAF College at Cranwell and the CFS. The type also briefly served with 24 (Communications) Squadron and was a favourite as a station flight aircraft at Andover, Bircham Newton, Biggin Hill, Boscombe Down, Donibristle, Duxford, Hal Far, Kenley, Mildenhall, Northolt, North Weald, Tangmere, Upavon, Upper Heyford and Worthy Down. The D.H.60M served briefly with 41, 601 and 604 Squadrons during the 1930s and with 501 Squadron from October 1942 until April 1944.

During the 1930 and 1931 RAF Hendon Air Displays, the instructors at the CFS gave a number of impressive performances of aerobatics and inverted flying. The first of these teams was led by Flt Lt J. S. Chick MC, AFC, while the 1931 season was led by Flt Lt B. E. Embry, AFC. When the new RAF Volunteer Reserve (RAFVR) schools began to open in 1937, the Gipsy Moth gave good service with 15 Elementary and Reserve Flying School (ERFTS) at Redhill and 17 ERFTS at Barton.

The first D.H.60M Gipsy Moth to enter RAF service was J9992, pictured with the A&AEE at Martlesham Heath during handling and spinning trials in the summer of 1929.

Production

In total, 136 Gipsy Moths were built between 1929 and March 1931, with the serials J9922 to J9932 (ordered to Contract 912850/29), K1103 to K1112 (Contract 932183/29, delivered between December 1929 and January 1930), K1198 to K1227 (Contract 5785/30, delivered between April and July 1930), K1241 (Contract 8660/30), K1825 to K1907 (Contract 27847/30 delivered between October 1930 and March 1931) and K2235 (Re-build from K1217 for RAE/Marine Aircraft Experimental Establishment (MAEE) central float trials).

Technical Data – D.H.60M Gipsy Moth	
ENGINE	One 120hp de Havilland Gipsy II
WINGSPAN	30ft
LENGTH	23ft 11in
HEIGHT	8ft 9½in
WING AREA	243sq/ft
EMPTY WEIGHT	900lb
LOADED WEIGHT	1,400lb
MAX SPEED	105mph at sea level
INITIAL CLIMB	700ft/min
CEILING	13,000ft
RANGE	230 miles

The last D.H.60M delivered to the RAF was K2235, which was actually a re-build from components donated by K1217, which was struck off charge (SOC) in 1931. Fitted with a central main float and wingtip floats, the aircraft was tested by the Marine Aircraft Experimental Establishment (MAEE) at Felixstowe between 1932 and 1936.

D.H.82 Tiger Moth

Development
Destined to serve the RAF for 23 years, the Tiger Moth has become one of the most famous training aircraft of all time and today is one of the most desired vintage aircraft around. Introduced in February 1932, the Tiger Moth was employed as the RAF's standard elementary trainer, and it remained in this vital role with Flying Training Command until 1947 and the RAFVR at Heany in southern Rhodesia until 1951. The very last biplane trainer to serve in the RAF, it was replaced by the Prentice and the highly successful Chipmunk.

Design
A development of the Gipsy Moth, the Tiger Moth was a two-seat elementary trainer made of a composite wood and metal construction covered in fabric. The aircraft differed in having staggered and swept-back wings, an inverted Gipsy Major engine and a number of minor improvements. The swept-back wings were incorporated to make it much easier to escape from the front cockpit in the event of an emergency, while the inverted engine improved forward vision. Fully certified for aerobatics up to a weight of 1,750lb, the Tiger Moth could also be equipped with a blind-flying hood for instrument instruction.

The first production Tiger Moths, the Mk Is, were installed with a 120hp Gipsy III, while the Mk IIs were powered by a 130hp Gipsy Major, which would become the standard production engine. The Mk IIs also differed from the original aircraft by having anti-spin strakes fitted to the tail unit.

Service
The prototype made its maiden flight on 26 October 1931, and was designed to Specification 23/31. The first batch of Mk Is joined the CFS and were in the public eye for the first time at the RAF Air Display at Hendon in 1932. From 1937 to 1939, the Tiger Moth equipped 44ERFTS and, by the outbreak of World War Two, the RAF had taken delivery of more than 1,000 examples.

Perfect for ab initio training, the vast majority of service pilots who trained during the war would have cut their teeth on the Tiger Moth before being posted on to a service FTS. During the early stages of the war, 28 flying schools operated the Tiger Moth in Britain, 25 in Canada, a dozen in Australia, seven in South Africa, five in Rhodesia and four in New Zealand. Post-war, 25 reserve flying schools and 18 university air squadrons retained the type until the last was retired in February 1955.

Production
There were 4,668 Tiger Moths built in Britain; 3,433 of them by Morris Motors Ltd, Cowley, between 1941 and 1945, and a further 2,751 were constructed in Australia, Canada and New Zealand.

D.H.82 Tiger Moth

Technical Data – D.H.82 Tiger Moth	
ENGINE	One 130hp de Havilland Gipsy Major I
WINGSPAN	29ft 4in
LENGTH	23ft 11in
HEIGHT	8ft 9½in
WING AREA	239sq/ft
EMPTY WEIGHT	1,115lb
LOADED WEIGHT	1,770lb
MAX SPEED	109mph at 1,000ft
INITIAL CLIMB	673 ft/min
CEILING	13,600ft
RANGE	302 miles
ENDURANCE	3 hrs

Above: The RAF ordered an initial production batch of 35 Tiger Moth Mk Is, which were powered by the 120hp Gipsy III engine, including K2579, pictured on 23 May 1932. The aircraft later settled with 24 Squadron, serving between October 1934 and October 1937.

Right: A large number of Tiger Moths were built and shipped to Australia during World War Two to equip 12 Elementary Flying Training Schools (EFTS), which provided ab initio training under the Empire Training Scheme.

Part of a batch of 400 Tiger Moth Mk IIs built by de Havilland at Hatfield, R5130 was typical of the breed, serving with eight different units until it was sold onto the civilian market in 1953 and re-registered G-APOV.

D.H.82B Queen Bee

Development
A derivative of the Tiger Moth and the Moth Major, the Queen Bee was initially designed to Specification 18/33, which called for a radio-controlled fleet gunnery target aircraft. On the surface, the aircraft looked very much like a Tiger Moth but actually only made use of the mainplanes and undercarriage and a few minor components.

Design
Other than those components mentioned, the Queen Bee used the same spruce and plywood fuselage of the Moth Major to keep the cost down and make the aircraft buoyant. The aircraft was powered by a Gipsy Major engine, effectively making the aircraft a Moth Major with Tiger Moth wings. The front cockpit was retained, complete with instruments and flying controls, but was faired over when in operation. The rear cockpit was covered by a piece of hinged decking to create a compartment for the Farnborough-designed radio equipment. Electric power for the equipment was provided by a wind-driven generator on the port side of the aircraft. A 25-gallon, rather than the standard 19-gallon, fuel tank was installed to improve range. In service, the Queen Bee was fitted with a pair of Short twin metal floats, and undercarriages were only installed for test flying or ferrying.

Service
The prototype, K3584, made its maiden flight ('manually' with a test pilot) from Hatfield on 5 January 1935. On 26 June, the seventh production aircraft, K4227, was tested for the first time using radio-control via a push button panel. The aircraft took-off, manoeuvred and was landed with little difficulty. Designed for a catapult take-off from either a ship- or a land-based catapult, the Queen Bee would fly a pre-determined course while trainee gunners tried to shoot it down. If they missed, the aircraft would be hoisted aboard a recovery ship and returned to the launch point.

A Queen Bee Flight was formed as 1 Anti-Aircraft Co-Operation Unit (AACU) at Henlow in May 1937 and the first operational flight was carried out from Watchett, on the Somerset coast, by K8661 in July. By 1941, the aircraft was being operated by T to Z Flights, 1 AACU, 2 AACU at Gosport and the Royal Navy's 3 and 4 AACUs based at Hal Far and Seletar. The Royal Navy operated the Queen Bee from August 1941 until February 1946, while the RAF declared its remaining stock obsolete on 12 November 1946.

Production
The production order for 380 aircraft was issued to Specification 20/35, made up of 320 Queen Bees built by de Havilland at Hatfield from 1935, and 60 by Scottish Aviation, Glasgow, during 1943 and 1944.

D.H.82B Queen Bee

Technical Data – D.H.82B Queen Bee	
ENGINE	One 130hp de Havilland Gipsy Major I
WINGSPAN	29ft 4in
LENGTH	23ft 11in
HEIGHT	8ft 9½in
WING AREA	239sq/ft
EMPTY WEIGHT	1,115lb
ALL-UP WEIGHT	1,825lb

Right: Queen Bee L5894 on a land-based catapult whilst serving with 1 Anti-Aircraft Co-operation Unit (AACU) from Manorbier on the Pembrokeshire Coast. A certain VIP appears to be more interested in the camera than the aircraft.

Below: K5059 'B' of 2 AACU in early 1937. The aircraft was damaged beyond repair on 8 June 1937, after accumulating 69.45 hours, which was quite high for a Queen Bee.

D.H.84M Dragon

Development
The original civilian D.H.84 Dragon came about because of Edward Hillman's (Hillman Airways) request for a twin-engined version of the D.H.83 Fox Moth for a new service from southern England to Paris. At the same time, the Iraqi Air Force also declared an interest in a similar aircraft and, even before a single machine had been built, the orders began to flow in.

Design
A straightforward design, the D.H.84 had a slab-sided plywood box fuselage, the same as the D.H.83. A twin-bay biplane, the wings could be folded to back, hinged outboard of the two 130hp Gipsy Major inline engines.

The militarised version of the aircraft was designated D.H.84M, and the first examples built for the Iraqi Air Force were the most aggressively equipped. Capable of carrying 16 x 20lb bombs, the Iraqi machines were installed with a pair of machine guns fitted into the nose and a third in a mid-upper position accessed via the rear of the cabin. A guard rail was installed to stop the rear gunner shooting off the aircraft's tail, which, on military variants, was distinguishable by a long curving dorsal fin.

Service
The first of eight D.H.84Ms were delivered to the Iraqi Air Force on 13 May 1933. The aircraft would carry out patrol duties and be employed very effectively for the suppression of local uprisings. In March 1934, a pair of D.H.84Ms was purchased for the Danish Army Air Force and, in 1937, the Portuguese Air Force also acquired three aircraft.

Several other nations impressed ex-civilian D.H.84s into service for military duties during World War Two, including the RAF. Seventeen D.H.84s were impressed into service to serve with several AACUs and 24 Squadron, although one, non-military conversion had served the military-operated King's Flight between 1933 and 1935.

In Australia, during the war, an urgent requirement for radio and navigation trainers prompted the de Havilland Aircraft Pty Ltd at Bankstown to put the D.H.84M back in production, despite the fact that the type had long been superseded by the D.H.89 Dragon Rapide. The reason for choosing the older design was that the 130hp Gipsy Major engine was still being produced in Australia for Tiger Moth construction. The Royal Australian Air Force (RAAF) took delivered of 87 D.H.84Ms, the first of them flying from Bankstown on 29 September 1942. The RAAF operated the type until 1947, when the survivors were sold onto the civilian market.

Production
There were 101 military D.H.84Ms built between 1933 and 1943. The first eight (Nos 16 to 21), built by de Havilland at Stag Lane, were for the Iraqi Air Force in 1933; two (S.21 and S.22) were for the Danish Army Air Force in 1934; and three for the Portuguese Air Force in 1937. There were 87 built by de Havilland Aircraft Pty Ltd at Bankstown, Sydney, for the RAAF between October 1942 and June 1943, serialled A34-12 to A34-98.

Technical Data – D.H.84M Dragon	
ENGINE	Two 130hp de Havilland Gipsy Major I
WINGSPAN	47ft 4in
LENGTH	34ft 6in
HEIGHT	10ft 1in
WING AREA	376sq/ft
EMPTY WEIGHT	2,300lb
ALL-UP WEIGHT	4,200lb
MAX SPEED	128mph
INITIAL CLIMB	612ft/min
CEILING	12,500ft
RANGE	460 miles
ARMAMENT	Three machine guns, two in the nose and one a mid-upper position, and up to 16 x 20lb bombs

The military D.H.84M was quite an elusive creature, hence the low-quality image of this example, which is in fact of the first aircraft for the Iraqi Air Force leaving Stag Lane on 13 May 1933.

D.H.86B

Development
The original D.H.86 airliner was designed in response to a QANTAS requirement for a multi-engined aircraft for services across the Timor Sea. Designed and built very quickly, the aircraft was subjected to a number of changes before it was accepted by a number of airlines.

Design
Of all-wood construction covered by fabric, the four-engined D.H.86 was an enlarged derivative of the Dragon Rapide. The prototype and the first two production aircraft were flown by a single pilot in a narrow cockpit, but both QANTAS and Imperial Airways required a two-pilot arrangement positioned side by side. All subsequent aircraft were modified to two pilot operations and consequently QANTAS, Imperial Airways and Jersey Airways placed their orders.

An improved D.H.86A followed in 1935, with a new windscreen, metal rudder, pneumatic undercarriage, larger brakes and tailwheel. Twenty of these were built and, later, a number of them were upgraded to D.H.86B standard, complete with auxiliary end plates to improve rudder and aileron control.

Service
The first D.H.86B to enter RAF service was ex-British Airways Ltd G-ADYI, which was re-serialled as L7596 and allocated to 24 (Communications) Squadron at Hendon in October 1937. Two further D.H.86Bs, again ex-British Airways, were purchased by the RAF, serialled L8037 and L8040 (ex-G-ADYC and G-ADYD, respectively) and were allocated to the E&WS at Cranwell in November 1937. The last of four D.H.86Bs purchased during the pre-war period was G-ADYG, which was given the military serial N6246 and joined L7596 in 24 Squadron in June 1938. Both of the Cranwell aircraft gave good service that continued with 24 Squadron and then a transfer to the FAA. L7596 was not so lucky; the aircraft was wrecked in a forced landing near Kirby-in-Furness on 28 July 1939, while N6246 was destroyed in a hangar fire at Hendon on 5 May 1942.

From April 1940, the first of 21 D.H.86As and Bs were impressed into military service. Out of this number, 11 served with the RAF at home, in the Middle East and India and five joined the FAA, all were delivered to Donibristle between April and July 1940; two served with the RAAF and two with the Royal New Zealand Air Force.

Production
Four D.H.86Bs were purchased by the RAF in 1937 and 1938 and a further 21 As and Bs were impressed between July 1940 and July 1942. The impressed aircraft were G-ACPL (HK844); G-ACWE (HX789); G-ACYG (AX840); G-ACZO (AX841); G-ACZP (AX843); G-ACZR (AX844); G-ADEA (A31-7); VH-UUB (A31-3); G-ADMY (X9442); G-ADFF (AX760); G-ADUE (AX762); G-ADUF (HK828); G-ADUG (HK831); G-ADUI (HK830); G-ADYI (AX795); G-AEAP (HK843); G-AEJM (X9441) and G-AENR (AX842); VH-USD (AX800); ZK-AEG (NZ552); and ZK-AEH (NZ553).

Technical Data – D.H.86B	
ENGINE	Four 200hp de Havilland Gipsy Six series I
WINGSPAN	64ft 6in
LENGTH	46ft 1in
HEIGHT	13ft
EMPTY WEIGHT	6,489lb
ALL-UP WEIGHT	10,420lb
MAX SPEED	166mph
INITIAL CLIMB	925ft/min
CEILING	17,400ft
RANGE	450–750 miles

The first D.H.86B to be delivered to the RAF was L7596 in October 1937, which was allocated to 24 (Communications) Squadron stationed at Hendon.

D.H.93 Don

Development
In 1936, the Air Ministry issued Specification T.6/36 for an advanced monoplane trainer capable of mounting a manually operated dorsal turret. The only other company to bid for the specification was Miles, with its M.9 Kestrel Trainer prototype, which would evolve into the successful Master family of trainers. While the Miles bid would clearly have its day under a separate specification, the de Havilland design was chosen for T.6/36.

Design
The D.H.93 Don was a three-seat, low wing monoplane with retractable undercarriage. Construction was of a wooden stressed skin, while power was provided by a 525hp Gipsy King 12-cylinder engine driving constant speed metal airscrew. The engine was neatly enclosed, and cooling was provided by a pair of intakes positioned in the leading edge of wing, directly above the undercarriage wells. The cockpit had dual controls for pilot training, a third seat to the rear within a spacious cabin for wireless operator training and a dorsal turret for gunnery training.

Service
The prototype D.H.93, with experimental serial E.3 (aka L2387) applied, made its maiden flight from Hatfield on 18 June 1937. On 26 June, the aircraft appeared at the RAF Display Hendon, where it was demonstrated by Flt Lt E. R. Symonds. The aircraft also appeared at the SBAC the following week.

Following early flight trials, it was found necessary to fit a pair of auxiliary fins under the tailplane of E.3 before the aircraft was delivered to the A&AEE for performance trials at Martlesham Heath. Having already received an order for 250 aircraft, de Havilland began production, only to be told that 'official policy' had changed, and the order was reduced to just 50. While the aircraft was found to be acceptable, further Air Ministry-sanctioned improvements proved too much for the airframe and de Havilland decided that the aircraft would be more useful as a communications aircraft. No turret was fitted to these machines and, once re-submitted to the A&AEE, a number entered service with a variety of units.

Out of the 50 that were built, the Don served with 24 Squadron (L2394) and the following Station Flights: Abingdon (L2400), Andover (L2395, L2399 and L2401), Eastchurch (L2392 and L2393), Grantham (L2390), Mildenhall (L2398), Northolt (L2403) and Wyton (L2396). The type also served with the EWS (L2407), the RAE (L2412) and 1 (L2413), 2 (L2415), 3 (L2414), 5 (L2419), 6 (L2418), 8 (L2420), 9 (L2416), 11 (L2421) and 13 FTS (L2428 to L2430). The bulk of the Dons were SOC on 17 March 1939, all of these being turned into instructional airframes, while the remainder were SOC four days later and all but three of this batch were scrapped.

Production
In total, 50 (L2387 to L2436) aircraft were all constructed at Hatfield to Contract No 539246/36 and were delivered between June 1937 and March 1939.

Technical Data – D.H.93 Don	
ENGINE	One 525hp de Havilland Gipsy King I
WINGSPAN	47ft 6in
LENGTH	37ft 4in
HEIGHT	9ft 5in
WING AREA	304sq/ft
EMPTY WEIGHT	5,050lb
ALL-UP WEIGHT	6,530lb
MAX SPEED	189mph at 3,750ft
INITIAL CLIMB	820ft/min
CEILING	21,500ft
RANGE	890 miles
ARMAMENT	One .303in machine gun in a dorsal turret

Right: The prototype, sporting experimental registration E.3, not long after the aircraft was rolled out in June 1937. Note the position of the dorsal turret, which at this stage was a mock-up. It was the increasing weight of the turret that forced de Havilland to redesign the aircraft for the communications role.

Below: The fifth production Don, after conversion to the 'more pleasing on the eye' communications version of the type, without the dorsal turret and raised rear fuselage. This aircraft, L2391, is pictured at Martlesham Heath but was wrecked there on 22 September 1938, after undershooting the runway; it was the only Don loss.

D.H.95 Flamingo

Development
Designed to compete against the all-dominating Douglas DC-3 and Lockheed Electra, the D.H.95 Flamingo showed great promise when it first appeared, but its civilian career was scuppered by the outbreak of World War Two.

Design
Ronald Eric Bishop's first design for de Havilland was also the company's first all-metal aircraft, the D.H.95 Flamingo. A good-looking machine, the Flamingo was a medium-range passenger transport capable of carrying between 12 and 17 passengers plus a crew of three, comprising, pilot, co-pilot and wireless operator. A high-wing, cantilever monoplane, power was provided by a pair of Bristol Perseus XIIC sleeve valve radials, driving de Havilland hydromatic three-blade propellers. Other 'modern' features included a hydraulically retractable undercarriage and split trailing edge flaps.

A one-off military version of the Flamingo named the Hertfordshire was built; the aircraft only differed from its civilian counterpart by its smaller oval cabin windows. Built to Specification 19/39, the production version of the Hertfordshire was to be capable of carrying up to 22 paratroops and an order for 30 aircraft was placed but later cancelled to enable the company to focus on Tiger Moth production.

Service
The first D.H.95 Flamingo (c/n 95001) made its maiden flight in the hands of Geoffrey de Havilland, Jr and George Gibbins from Hatfield on 22 December 1938. During early flight trials, it was found that a third central fin was needed, but production aircraft had their two original fins enlarged with larger area, horn-balanced rudders.

The Air Ministry was very impressed with the performance of the Flamingo and its potential as a military transport. Allocated the serial T5357, which was not displayed, the aircraft was evaluated in March 1939, by which time civilian interest was growing. Orders were placed by the Egyptian government and by Guernsey and Jersey Airways Ltd, which carried out route proving trials with the prototype in May 1939, lasting two months. Two aircraft were ordered by the latter airline but, by the time they were ready, the war had begun, and they were impressed into military service instead.

In RAF service, the type served with 24 Squadron, the King's Flight and a single example gave good service to 782 Squadron, operating out of Donibristle until mid-1944. The latter was originally allocated to BOAC, which ordered eight Flamingos, the type serving from Cairo for duties throughout the Middle East until they were withdrawn in 1943, destined never to serve again.

The ex-782 Squadron aircraft, BT312, named *Merlin VI* (later *Merlin 27*), re-registered as G-AFYH, was the only example of a Flamingo to serve during the post-war period with British Air Transport Ltd. The aircraft only served between 1945 and 1946 and was scrapped at Redhill in 1954.

Production
Fourteen D.H.95 Flamingos were built, along with a single D.H.95 Hertfordshire, serialled R2510, which was built to Contract 97/39 (later B.8999/39) and delivered to the RAF in June 1940.

D.H.95 Flamingo

Technical Data – D.H.95 Flamingo	
ENGINE	Two 930hp Bristol Perseus XVI
WINGSPAN	70ft
LENGTH	51ft 7in
HEIGHT	15ft 3in
WING AREA	651sq/ft
EMPTY WEIGHT	11,325lb
ALL-UP WEIGHT	18,000lb
MAX SPEED	239mph
INITIAL CLIMB	1,470ft/min
CEILING	20,900ft
RANGE	1,210 miles

A one-off event photograph of the sole Hertfordshire, R2510, nearest to the camera, with prototype T5357 in the lead, followed by R2764 and AE444 in the distance.

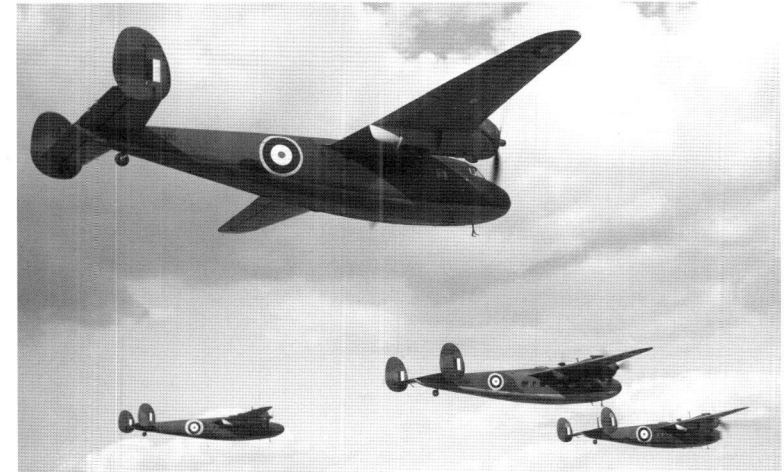

Flamingo G-AGCC (aka R2766) was on standby in 1940 in case it was needed to evacuate the royal family in the event of an invasion. Later allocated to 24 (Communications) Squadron in February 1941, the aircraft was re-named *Lady of Glamis* in 1942.

D.H.89M and D.H.89B Dominie Mk I and II

Development
While the Dragon Rapide was a development of the Dragon, the Dominie was a militarised version of the former. A huge success during the 1930s, the Rapide family of aircraft helped to introduce a large number of small independent airlines, thanks to the aircraft's economic performance. The Rapide also saw military service, initially in competition with the Anson, for Specification 18/35 for a new general reconnaissance aircraft. Designated the DH.89M, the aircraft was beaten by the Anson but, not long after, was adopted as a communications aircraft; the first examples joined 24 Squadron at Hendon in 1938.

Design
It was in 1939 that the Air Ministry ordered a new radio trainer version of the Rapide to Specification 29/38. Intended for service with the RAF's E&WS, the aircraft was designated as the D.H.89B and was initially produced in two variants, simply known as the Mk I and Mk II. The service name of 'Dominie' was not adopted until January 1941.

Construction was a traditional wooden, fabric-covered structure with power provided by a pair of 200hp Gipsy Queen engines. The Mk I was a five- or six-seat radio or navigation trainer distinguishable by a direction-finding loop, while the Mk II was a ten-seat communications aircraft.

Service
The D.H.89B was first delivered to the RAF in September 1939 and was destined to serve until June 1955, when the type was declared as obsolete. As well as its intended core duty of training wireless operators, the Dominie carried out a wide range of communications roles, including sterling service with the Air Transport Auxiliary (ATA).

Just like the RAF, the FAA adopted a large number of impressed Rapides and also took delivery of 63 Dominie Mk Is and IIs between 1940 and 1945. The bulk of FAA Dominies were retired by 1946, but a handful served on operationally, the last with 1844 Squadron at Hal Far, Malta, which were not retired until March 1957, when the unit was disbanded. However, even as late as 1961, 14 were still on FAA charge and three (NF847, NF867 and NF881) remained airworthy for experience flights.

The Dominie and Rapide also served with more than 20 different foreign air forces, the Dutch being one of the last to retire their examples in 1956.

Production
A total of 469 Dominies were built for the RAF; 186 of these were built by de Havilland at Hatfield (R5921 to R5954 and X7320 to X7525). The remainder were built by Brush Coachworks at Loughborough from 1942 (HG664 to HG732, NF847 to NF853 and RL936 to RL946). The last Dominie was delivered in July 1946.

Technical Data – D.H.89B Dominie Mk I and II	
ENGINE	Two 200hp de Havilland Gipsy Queen 3
WINGSPAN	48ft
LENGTH	34ft 6in
HEIGHT	10ft 3in
WING AREA	340sq/ft
EMPTY WEIGHT	3,230lb
ALL-UP WEIGHT	5,500lb
MAX SPEED	157mph at 1,000ft
INITIAL CLIMB	867ft/min
CEILING	16,700ft
RANGE	570 miles

Right: The interior of Dominie Mk I radio trainer in a five-seat configuration. Hundreds, if not thousands, of RAF wireless operators learned their trade on the Dominie.

Below: One of the last military Dominies to remain in service was NF881, which was not SOC until 22 June 1963. The aircraft served on in 'civvie' street with the Anglo Diesel Company.

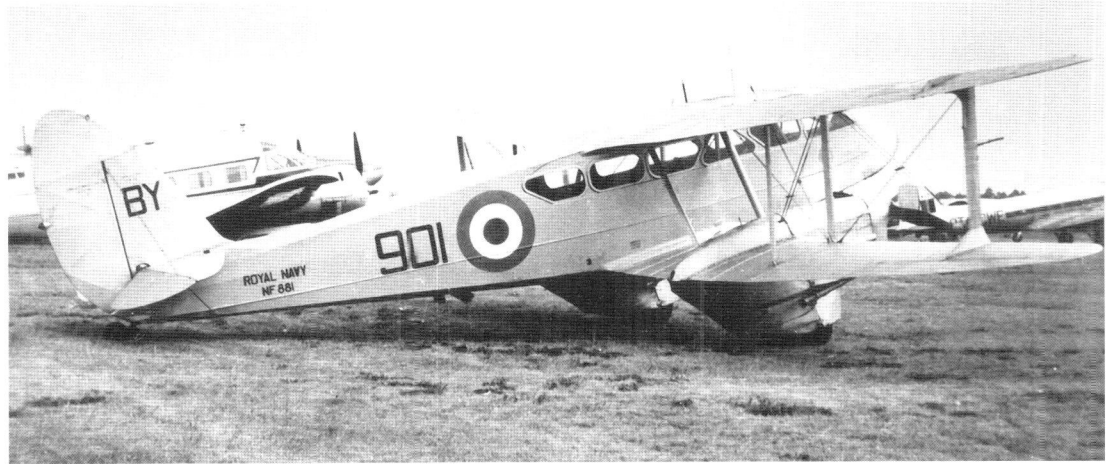

De Havilland D.H.89B Dominie Mk I X7398 of No 2 Radio School stationed at Yatesbury.

D.H.98 Mosquito (Bomber)

Development
After beginning official flight trials from February 1941, the prototype Mosquito B Mk IV, W4057, was in the air by September. Nine B Mk IV Series 1s followed (W4064–W4072), all of which were completed by February 1942, and a further 300 B Mk IV Series 2 had left the Hatfield factory by September 1943.

Design
The B Mk IV was the first 'light' bomber variant of the Mosquito to enter squadron service, only differing from the original specification in carrying four 500lb bombs (later increased to 4,000lb with the addition of bulged bomb bay doors), twice the load that was originally planned.

Service
The Mosquito B Mk IV entered service with 2 (Light Bomber) Group, replacing the Blenheim, which had been taking a pasting, especially during low-level daylight operations. 105 Squadron at Swanton Morley was to be the first recipient from November 1941. The squadron carried out its first operation, a daylight attack on Cologne on 31 May 1942, the day after the city was struck by the first 'thousand-bomber' raid.

Mosquitoes flew operationally for 2 Group between May 1942 and May 1943, carrying out over 100 successful daylight raids with a much lower loss rate and considerably more clout than the Blenheim before it. By June 1942, 105 Squadron, which had moved to Marham, was joined by 139 (Jamaica) Squadron. One of 105 Squadron's raids that made the headlines was the daring attack on the Gestapo headquarters in Oslo on 25 September 1942. Operating at an exceptionally low-level, 2 Group employed a 'low-level formation' and a 'shallow-diver formation' to achieve its goals. Both formations flew a co-ordinated attack. The 'shallow-divers' came in at 2,000ft and dropped their bombs at 1,500ft, while the 'low-levellers' came in straight at the target as low as possible.

Variants
B Mk V was a development of the B Mk IV, with a new 'standard wing' capable of carrying a pair of 50-gallon jettisonable fuel tanks or a pair of 500lb bombs and was a prototype for the Canadian-built B Mk VII. The first batch of Canadian-built Mosquitoes were B Mk VIIs, based on the B Mk V and powered by the Merlin 31 engine, the first flight of them flew from Toronto on 24 September 1942. B Mk IX, a high-altitude unarmed bomber, without a pressurised cabin, powered by a pair of Merlin 72 engines, was capable of carrying four 500lb bombs in the bay and two more under each wing. B Mk XVI, was as per the B Mk IX, but with a pressurised cabin and powered by the Merlin 72, 73, 76 or 77 engines. It was capable of carrying 3,000lb of bombs but, by 1944, all were converted to carry 4,000lb bombs; 529 were built. B Mk XX, was as per the B Mk VII but furnished with Canadian/American equipment and powered by Packard Merlin 31 or 33 engines. The first two aircraft (KB162 and KB328) were delivered to Britain via Greenland in August 1943 and, by late November, were operational. The first B Mk XX operation was flown by 139 Squadron when KB161 bombed Berlin on 2 December 1943. Forty B Mk XXs were modified with aerial cameras, delivered to the USAAF and re-designated as the F.8 for meteorological and reconnaissance duties. B.23 was a development of the B Mk XX powered by Merlin 69 engines instead of the Merlin 255

in case supplies should run low. B.25 was as per the Canadian-built B Mk XX, but powered by Merlin 225 engines. B.35 was basically a B.XVI, but powered by Merlin 114 engines in the early production aircraft and Merlin 114A in the later.

Technical Data – D.H.98 Mosquito B Mk IV	
ENGINE	Two 1,460hp Rolls-Royce Merlin 21 and 23
WINGSPAN	54ft 2in
LENGTH	40ft 6in
HEIGHT	12ft 6in
WING AREA	454sq/ft
EMPTY WEIGHT	13,400lb
ALL-UP WEIGHT	21,462lb
MAX SPEED	380mph
INITIAL CLIMB	2,500ft/min
CEILING	34,000ft
RANGE	2,040 miles

Right: A Mosquito B.IV of 105 Squadron at Marham in late 1942 awaiting its load of four 500lb bombs.

Below: Several B.IVs that were still in service were converted to carry a single 4,000lb 'cookie' by fitting bulged bomb-bays. This is DZ594 during trials with the A&AEE; the aircraft later joined 627 Squadron before being SOC on 28 June 1945.

D.H.98 Mosquito (Night Fighter)

Development
From the outset, interest from the Air Ministry, which originally ordered the Mosquito as a light bomber, quickly switched in favour of the fighter variant. Even by 1940, the original contract for 50 bombers was modified to 30 fighters and 20 bombers.

Design
Externally, the fighter variant did not differ a great deal from the bomber but, under the skin, modifications included a much stronger main wing spar to help deal with the higher loads experienced during combat and the nose being changed to accommodate four 20mm cannon and four .303in machine guns. The windscreen was also changed to a flat (later bulletproof) type and access to the cockpit was changed from the floor, as per the bomber, to a hatch-door on the starboard side of the fuselage.

The last of the three prototypes, W4052, was equipped as a night fighter as per Air Ministry Specification F.21/40 and designated the Mosquito NF.II, and first flew from a meadow behind Salisbury Hall on 15 May 1941. W4052 was fitted with the very latest radar equipment available, the AI Mk IV, which was specifically designed for intercepting enemy bombers at night. Its installation was characterised by its 'bow-and-arrow' aerial in the nose.

Service
The first of 398 Mosquito NF.IIs built entered service with Fighter Command from January 1942; the type steadily replaced the Beaufighter and the Havoc. 157 Squadron at Castle Camps was the first unit to receive the NF.II, followed by 23 Squadron at Ford, and, on 27/28 April, the first operational night sortie was flown. By the end of the year, 23 Squadron was moved to Luqa where, on 30/31 December, the first night intruder operation over the Mediterranean was flown. Between January and March 1943, 23 Squadron shot down 17 enemy aircraft and quickly became adept at shooting up trains in Italy, North Africa and Sicily.

A development of the FB.IV saw the arrival of the NF.XIII, which introduced the soon-to-be-familiar 'bull' nose around the AI Mk VIII radar. The next night fighter variant, the NF.XVII, was converted from the NF.II; it was very similar to the NF.XII but was the first of its kind to be fitted with the American AI Mk X centimetric radar. There were 99 NF.XVIIs built, and the first of them joined 25 Squadron in December 1943. It was Flt Lt Singleton and his navigator, Flt Lt G. Haslam, who, in HK255, shot down three Ju 188s in a single sortie on 19 March 1944, firmly endorsing 25 Squadron's new choice of aircraft.

The NF.XVII was superseded by the Merlin 25-powered NF.XIX, which entered service in May 1944 with 257 Squadron. The last Mosquito night fighter variant to see service during the war was the NF.XXX. By May 1945, seven RAF squadrons were tasked with home defence with 11 and 12 Group Fighter Command and a further three squadrons, with 100 Group, were still in service.

Nocturnal 'Mossie', post-war
Two further night fighter marks were destined to see service with the post-war RAF, the first of them was the NF.36; the prototype, RK955, first flew in May 1945. The very final night fighter variant and the last of all of the Mosquitoes to be built was the NF.38, which flew for the first time on 18 November 1947. Very similar to

the NF.36, the only major difference was a British AI Mk IX radar. All 101 NF.38s were built either at Hatfield or Chester, and the very last of them, VX916, left the Chester factory in November 1950; it was the last of 6,439 built in Britain and the last of the total 7,781 built, including Australian and Canadian production.

Technical Data – D.H.98 Mosquito NF.II	
ENGINE	Two 1,460hp Rolls-Royce Merlin 21 and 23
WINGSPAN	54ft 2in
LENGTH	40ft 6in
HEIGHT	12ft 6in
WING AREA	454sq/ft
EMPTY WEIGHT	13,431lb
ALL-UP WEIGHT	18,547lb
MAX SPEED	370mph
INITIAL CLIMB	3,000ft/min
CEILING	36,000ft
RANGE	1,705 miles

Right: A de Havilland Mosquito NF.II unleashes hell during a night firing test of its four 20mm cannons and four .303in machine guns simultaneously.

Below: The third production Mosquito NF.36, RK957, pictured at Boscombe Down during trials in May 1945. After this brief spell with the A&AEE, RK957 served with 141 Squadron and 228 Operational Conversion Unit, and remained in service until 21 March 1955.

D.H.98 Mosquito (Photo Reconnaissance)

Development

When the Mosquito was introduced in 1940, there was not an aircraft serving operationally in the world that came close to the performance figures being achieved by the de Havilland aircraft. Photographic reconnaissance (PR) was a high-priority tasking for the Mosquito and, even before the type left the drawing board, this role had already been allocated to one of the three prototypes, W4051.

The Mosquito would go on to become the RAF's main, long-range PR aircraft, serving extensively over Europe, Burma and the South Pacific. With the end of the war, there was no let-up in the type's tasking in the photographic role, and it was not until the arrival of the Canberra PR.3 that the later marks began to be replaced, although several remained in RAF service in the Far East until late 1955.

Service

The PR.I prototype, W4051, first flew on 10 June 1941 and, after trials and evaluation at the A&AEE, the aircraft was transferred to the Photographic Reconnaissance Unit (PRU), later 1 PRU, at Benson. Only ten PR.Is were built, including the prototype. All initially joined 1 PRU and, of those that survived that tour of duty, they later served with 69, 521 or 540 Squadron.

The very first successful operation was flown on 20 September 1941 by W4055 of 1 PRU, in daylight, photographing enemy facilities at Brest, La Pallice and Bordeaux before running for home via Paris. The Mosquito did attract the attention of the enemy, which despatched three Bf 109s to deal with the intruder, but none of the enemy fighters came close.

Bomber Command was one of 1 PRU's biggest customers, with requests for target photography both in planning a raid and once the attack was over for post-raid analysis. The locations of enemy warships, especially when they were poised in Atlantic ports, was another favourite Mosquito PR target and so were enemy radar stations; prior to D-Day, more than 70 had been photographed and pinpointed thanks to PR sorties.

By late 1942, 1 PRU could no longer cope alone with the workload, so it was rapidly expanded and divided into four squadrons. Two of them, 540 and 544 Squadron, were equipped with Mosquitoes and, from late 1943, 140 Squadron was re-equipped too.

With the arrival of the high-altitude B.IX in RAF service, it was a logical step to produce a PR version, which saw the introduction of the backbone Mosquito recce aircraft, the PR.IX, in May 1943. It entered service with 540 Squadron.

The final wartime-built Mosquito PR was another development of the PR.XVI, the PR.34, which was effectively a very long-range version. Post-war, the PR.34 became the most common type in service with the PR squadrons until the type's withdrawal. Many were upgraded to PR.34A standard by Marshalls of Cambridge Ltd; this involved fitting a pair of Merlin 114A engines, new Gee equipment and a better retraction system for the undercarriage.

The last Mosquito PR was a conversion of the B.35 bomber. The PR.35 was specifically designed for night-time PR operations using powerful photoflashes. Only six were converted, all by de Havilland at its Leavesden plant.

D.H.98 Mosquito (Photo Reconnaissance)

Technical Data – D.H.98 Mosquito PR.1	
ENGINE	Two 1,460hp Rolls-Royce Merlin 21 and 23
WINGSPAN	54ft 2in
LENGTH	40ft 6in
HEIGHT	12ft 6in
WING AREA	454sq/ft
EMPTY WEIGHT	12,824lb
ALL-UP WEIGHT	19,670lb
MAX SPEED	382mph
INITIAL CLIMB	2,850ft/min
CEILING	35,000ft
RANGE	2,180 miles

Above: PR.IV DZ383 pictured at Boscombe Down during trials. The ex-B.IV is resplendent in 'PR Blue' and the port rear facing oblique camera port can just be seen behind the engine nacelle.

Right: NS504 from 540 Squadron pictured in June 1944, hence the invasion stripes. Only weeks after this photograph was taken, the PR.XVI failed to return from an operation to Lyon on 6 August 1944.

RG245, a PR.34 from 540 Squadron, presents us with a rare air-to-air view of a Mosquito PR's camera ports in 1948. The aircraft also briefly served with 58 Squadron until coming to grief with 540 Squadron at Benson after it swung on take-off on 5 April 1950.

D.H.98 Mosquito (Trainers and Tugs)

Development
From the outset, the design of the Mosquito made it the most suitable for conversion to a trainer, unlike many other military aircraft during World War Two that launched the trainee pilot into the 'wild blue' without the comfort of an instructor beside them.

Design
The Mosquito T Mk III was fitted with dual controls, not fitted with armament and powered by Merlin 21, 23 or 25 engines. Fully loaded, complete with a pair of 100-gallon drop tanks, the T Mk III weighed in at 20,319lb. The prototype was W4053, which first flew in the hands of Geoffrey de Havilland from Hatfield on 30 January 1942.

The T Mk III was not the only trainer version of the Mosquito. In Canada, the T.22 was produced, which was based on the FB.21. The dual-controlled aircraft was powered by a pair of Packard-Merlin 33 engines. Only six T.22s were built: KA873 to KA876 and KA896 and KA897. De Havilland Canada also built the T.27, which was a development of the T.22, powered by Packard-Merlin 225 engines. Nineteen were built: KA877 to KA895. In Australia, a trainer was produced from the FB.40, which was designated the T.43. The Mosquito only differed from the fighter bomber by having dual controls and dual elevator trim tabs. Twenty-two were built.

Modified from the B.35, 27 Mosquitoes, the vast majority from storage, were converted into target tugs and re-designated the TT.35 by Brooklands Aviation Ltd at Sywell. The main modification was the fitment of an ML Type G wind-driven target winch under the fuselage.

Service
The first unit to receive the T Mk III was the Mosquito Conversion Unit (MCU, later re-designated as 1655 Mosquito Training Unit [MTU]), which was formed at Horsham St Faith in August 1942 but had moved to Marham by the end of the following month. By October, several were already arriving on operational units, including night fighter squadrons that used them to convert Beaufighter crews to the Mosquito without them leaving the unit. Operational Training Units (OTUs) were the next in line to receive the T Mk III in bulk; 60 OTU, which had reformed at High Ercall, was first and, later in the war, 8, 13, 16, 51 and 54 OTU also received the type.

Post-war, the type was still prevalent with Flying Training Command and formed the backbone of 204 Advanced Flying School (AFS), which was established at Cottesmore on 15 March 1947, until it was moved to Bassingbourn to become 'D' Flight of 231 Operational Conversion Unit (OCU) in February 1952.

TT.35s mainly served with the Civilian Anti-Aircraft Co-Operation Units (CAACUs), as well as the several OCUs and Target Towing Flights (TTFs). The RAF's TT.35s were the final Mosquitoes to serve, the last of which retired in 1956.

Production
In total, 362 Mosquito T.IIIs were built; all but 78 of them were built at Leavesden and the remainder at Hatfield. The type served with a host of squadrons, training units, wings and station flights until it was retired in 1953.

Technical Data – D.H.98 Mosquito T Mk III	
ENGINE	Two 1,460hp Rolls-Royce Merlin 21, 23 or 25
WINGSPAN	54ft 2in
LENGTH	40ft 6in
HEIGHT	12ft 6in
WING AREA	454sq/ft
EMPTY WEIGHT	13,104lb
ALL-UP WEIGHT	16,883lb
MAX SPEED	384mph
INITIAL CLIMB	2,500ft/min
CEILING	37,500ft
RANGE	1,560 miles

Right: Built as a B.35, RS719 only served with the Empire Test Pilot School (ETPS) before being converted to a TT.35. The aircraft went on to serve the Telecommunications Research Establishment (TRE), A&AEE, 3 Civilian Anti-Aircraft Co-Operation Unit (CAACU), the Temperature and Humidity (THUM) Flight at Woodvale and, finally, 5 CAACU before being SOC on 31 May 1958.

Below: The pilots of 3 CAACU at Exeter, pictured not long after the unit was formed on 18 March 1951, in front of a Mosquito TT.35. On 1 July 1954, the unit was amalgamated with 4 CAACU to become 3/4 CAACU. Chief Pilot Harry Ellis is in the middle of the front row.

D.H.98 Mosquito (Fighter Bomber)

Development
The most significant development of the NF.II was the FB.VI, which, as a fighter bomber, was destined to become the most used Mosquito fighter of all. The prototype FB.VI, HJ662, first flew on 1 June 1942, but, while nearing the end of successful flight trials with the A&AEE, an engine cut on take-off and the fighter was wrecked after hitting a pair of Beaufighters on the ground.

Design
The first 300 FB.VIs that were built were dedicated fighter bombers and were given the additional designation Series 1. These were designed to carry a pair of 250lb bombs at the rear of the bomb-bay and one under each wing, as well as retaining four .303in machine guns and four 20mm cannons in the nose. The Series 2 went one stage further by raising the armament to a pair of 500lb bombs in the rear bomb-bay and two more under each wing; the standard nose armament was retained.

Service
The FB.VI entered Fighter Command service in the role of day and night intruder and would later become a specialist at Ranger and Instep patrols. The Mosquito took over from the Boston III as an intruder, joining 418 Squadron at Ford in May 1943. From December, the FB.VI was also serving Coastal Command, progressively replacing the Beaufighter in the anti-shipping role and becoming a particularly useful platform for delivering unguided rocket projectiles (RPs).

The FB.VI was very successful in the anti-shipping role, achieving notoriety with the Banff Strike Wing for despatching enemy shipping along the Norwegian coast from September 1944 through to the end of the war. Armed with eight 60lb RPs plus the standard nose guns, the firepower of the FB.VI was estimated to be the same as a broadside from a 10,000-ton cruiser! Another version, the FB.XVIII, was fitted with a 57mm Molins gun; the prototype, HJ732, first flew on 8 June 1943, and all of the 20 that were built joined 248 Squadron from October 1943.

The Mosquito FB.VI also saw extensive service with the RAF's HD night fighter squadrons, as well as continuing to intrude deep over Germany. A 605 Squadron crew achieved the type's 100th enemy victory over Fassberg on 24 December 1943. As if to demonstrate the unit's wide area of operations, 605 Squadron achieved its 101st victory over London on 10/11 January 1944, when a Ju 188 was brought down in Germany's 'Little Blitz'.

Variants
The FB.VI was a development of the NF.II, with the same armament and an additional pair of 50-gallon wing tanks or two 500lb bombs. From 1944, aircraft were modified to carry four 60lb RPs under each wing instead of wing tanks. FB.XVIII was a development of the FB.VI, with a modified nose to accommodate a 6lb (57mm) Molins anti-tank gun in place of the standard four 20mm cannons; 20 were built. FB.21 was as per a DH-built FB.VI, of which only three were built; two were powered by Packard Merlin 31 engines and the other by Merlin 33s. FB.24 was a high-altitude development of the FB.21, powered by two-stage, supercharged Merlin 301 engines; only one was built. FB.26, another development of the FB.VI, this time powered by Merlin 225

engines and furnished with Canadian/American equipment. Designed to replace the FB.21, 398 FB.26s were built. FB.40, an Australian-built version of the FB.VI, was fitted with de Havilland hydromatic or Hamilton Standard propellers. The first of 178 FB.40s that were built flew from Sydney on 23 July 1943. The first 100 were powered by Merlin 31 engines and the remainder by Merlin 33s. FB.42, a single aircraft, ex-FB.40, was modified with Merlin 69 engines but the idea was shelved, and the Mosquito became the prototype PR.41.

Technical Data – D.H.98 Mosquito FB.VI	
ENGINE	Two 1,230hp Rolls-Royce Merlin 21 or 1,635hp Merlin 25
WINGSPAN	54ft 2in
LENGTH	40ft 6in
HEIGHT	12ft 6in
WING AREA	435sq ft
EMPTY WEIGHT	14,300lb
ALL-UP WEIGHT	22,300lb
MAX SPEED	380mph at 13,000ft
INITIAL CLIMB	7min to 15,000ft
CEILING	33,000ft
RANGE	1,205 miles or 1,705 miles with underwing tanks
ARMAMENT	(Series 2) Four 20mm guns and four .303in guns forward and two 500lb bombs in fuselage and two 500lb bombs or eight RPs under the wings

Armourers hard at work loading rocket projectiles (RPs) onto Mosquito FB.VI PZ438 at Banff in February 1945. This aircraft was brought down by flak over Ålesund on 17 March 1945.

248 Squadron converted from the Beaufighter X to the Mosquito FB.VI in June 1943, which was joined by the FB.XVIII in January 1944. At the time of the D-Day landings, when this shot was taken, this aircraft, NT225, was operating from Portreath.

D.H.98 Sea Mosquito

Development
The Royal Navy had been operating various marks of Mosquito from not long after its introduction into RAF service. At this stage, the aircraft was firmly land-based, but plans were evolving that would enable the Mosquito to be operated from a carrier in a front-line, operational capacity. Despite the success of the aircraft carrier trials that followed, the Mosquito was never adopted for operations at sea, but this did not stop three dedicated Sea Mosquito marks from being produced.

Service
The TR.33 served with nine FAA units between April 1946 and October 1950, all but one of them in a front-line capacity. Only 811 Squadron, which had reformed at Ford on 15 September 1945 with Mosquito FB.VIs would receive the TR.33 from April 1946. A dozen were taken on strength but, by the time the squadron moved to Brawdy in December 1946, half of them had already been withdrawn. Following another move to Eglinton in March 1947, the TR.33's brief operational career came to an end when 811 Squadron was disbanded on 1 July 1947.

One interesting task carried out by a pair of TR.33s, TW228 and TW230, was their part in the secretive Highball trials. These two aircraft were the only Sea Mosquitoes allocated to an RAF unit, namely the Highball Trials Flight, at Coningsby in Lincolnshire. The Highball bouncing bomb, designed by Barnes Wallis, had been in development since late 1942, with much of the work being carried out by the Mosquito-equipped 618 Squadron. The officially named flight, however, only existed from January 1946 to November 1947.

The last TR.33s served the FAA until June 1953 with 751 Squadron at Watton in Norfolk. Fifty-three were built in the serial ranges LR359, LR387, TS444, TS449, TW227–TW257 and NS586–NS589. The TR.37 was virtually identical to the TR.33, with the exception of the radar, which gave the aircraft a 'bull' type nose. The reason for this was that the American radar was replaced by the British ASV Mk 13B. Only 14 TR.37s were built, in the serial range VT724–VT727, and the type only served with 703 and 771 Squadrons between December 1948 and May 1950.

A derivative of the B.XVI, the target-towing TT.39 was converted by General Aircraft Ltd. Work included extending the forward fuselage into a glazed nose for a camera operator and the fitment of a dorsal glazed observation cupola. Some of the 35 aircraft were converted and re-fitted with Merlin 72/73 engines, and the nose modification extended the fuselage to a length of 43ft 4in. While the RAF continued to fly its dedicated TT.35s until 1956, only three squadrons of the FAA operated the TT.39 until May 1952. The final unit, 728 Squadron, retired the type at Hal Far, Malta.

Technical Data – D.H.98 Sea Mosquito TR.33

ENGINE	Two 1,705hp Rolls-Royce Merlin 66
WINGSPAN	54ft 2in
LENGTH	40ft 6in
HEIGHT	12ft 6in
WING AREA	454sq/ft
EMPTY WEIGHT	14,850lb
ALL-UP WEIGHT	23,850lb
MAX SPEED	376mph
INITIAL CLIMB	1,820ft/min
CEILING	30,100ft
RANGE	1,265 miles

Right: The Sea Mosquito TR.33 loaded and folded. This photograph of the prototype shows the four-bladed airscrews, the slinging of the 18in torpedo, and, on the folded wings, the 50-gallon drop tanks for which bombs may be substituted. The standard D.H. undercarriage is replaced by Lockheed hydraulic legs on the production aircraft.

Below: Ex-B.XVI PF606, following conversion to a TT.39 by Genera Aircraft Ltd. The aircraft survived until it was SOC at Lossiemouth on 27 November 1952.

D.H.100 Vampire F.1 and 2

Development
In April 1944, the Spider Crab was officially renamed the Vampire and, by the following month, a production order for 120 F.1s was placed with de Havilland. However, Hatfield was already snowed under with increased Mosquito production, and the very first Vampires that were built were sub-contracted to English Electric at Preston. The Lancashire-based aircraft manufacturer was selected because of its excellent efficiency in producing the Handley Page Hampden and Halifax. Work began at the Strand Road Factory in Preston, and on 24 May 1944, all Vampires were assembled and ready to be test flown from Samlesbury. The first production aircraft, TG274, flew from Samlesbury on 20 April 1945 and, three days later, was delivered to Hatfield for manufacturer's trials.

Design
To speed up the Vampire's entry into service, the first 50 that were built were not fitted with a pressurised cockpit. A planned cockpit heating seating was also not fitted; instead, warm air was extracted from a heater muff on the jet pipe via the gun heating system. The F.1 was armed with four 20mm Hispano Mk V cannons mounted below the fuselage with provision for 150rpg (rounds per gun). From the 50th aircraft (TG336) onwards, cabin pressurisation was installed with air supplied to the cockpit by a Marshall Type 6 blower while the canopy was kept airtight by a Dunlop seal. The first 40 F.1s built were fitted with a Goblin 1 but, from TG314 onwards, a 3,100lb Goblin 2 was installed.

A separate chain of Nene-powered Vampires was born when three F.1 airframes were converted to Specification F.11/45. The Nene was heavier than the Goblin but produced more power and, initially, the 4,500lb Nene RB.41 was installed by Rolls-Royce at Hucknall in 1945. Designated as the F.2, the aircraft was easily recognisable because of the Nene's need for extra airflow, which was provided by a pair of prominent 'elephant's ears' auxiliary intakes on top of the fuselage.

A production order for 60 F.2s was placed by the RAF, but this had been cancelled by September 1945. Development work of the Nene-powered Vampire did not go to waste, as both Australia and France would produce their own variants.

Service
The Vampire F.1 entered RAF service with 247 Squadron in March 1946 at Chilbolton, replacing the Tempest F.2. The unit worked up quickly on its new jet fighters and took part in the Victory Flypast over London on 8 June. In October 1946, 54 Squadron, another Tempest F.2 unit, received the Vampire F.1, followed by 72 Squadron, which was reformed at Odiham on 1 February 1947; the two units created the RAF's first Vampire Wing. The first Vampires to see service outside the country belonged to 3 Squadron at Wünstorf, West Germany, which relinquished its Tempest Vs for F.1s in April 1948. The Royal Auxiliary Air Force, which was destined to operate all marks of Vampire in large numbers, received its first in July 1948, when 605 (County of Warwick) Squadron, stationed at Honiley, replaced the Mosquito NF.30.

The Vampire F.1 served for a relatively short period of time with 12 operational squadrons between March 1946 and June 1951 but was gainfully employed with second line units into the mid-1950s. Such was the Vampire's pace of development that the much-improved F.3 was in service a little over of two years after the F.1.

Technical Data – DH.100 Vampire F.1 and 2	
ENGINE	(1) 3,100lb Goblin & Goblin 2; (2) 4,500lb Nene RB.41
WINGSPAN	40ft
LENGTH	30ft 9in
HEIGHT	8ft 10in
WING AREA	256sq/ft
WEIGHT	(1) 6,372lb; (2) 7,762lb
ALL-UP WEIGHT	(1) 10,298lb; (2) 13,448lb
MAX SPEED	(1) 540mph; (2) 575mph
CEILING	(1) 40,000ft; (2) 49,000ft
RANGE	(1) 730 miles; (2) 1,118 miles
ARMAMENT	Four 20mm Hispano Mk V cannons

The fifth production Vampire F.1, TG278, built at Preston and first flown from Samlesbury, en-route to Hatfield, photographed from an Albemarle in August 1945. De Havilland converted the Vampire to carry aerial cameras for a proposed photographic reconnaissance variant and later for Ghost engine development trials.

D.H.100 Vampire F.3

Development
The Vampire F.1 suffered from the same age-old problem that had plagued interceptors from the outset – endurance. The F.1 could only remain airborne, on average, for 45 minutes, although, with a pair of underwing tanks, this could be raised to two hours.

Design
This problem was tackled in June 1945, when Vampire F.1 TG275 was delivered to Hatfield for installation trials under 'Modification Number 15.' This modification involved fitting a new, long-range wing that increased the fighter's internal fuel capacity to 330 gallons. This was achieved by adding four extra fuel tanks in the outer wing and this added 128 gallons. The original inner wing fuel tanks were also upgraded to the Marston bag-type, as were the additional tanks.

A new type of external, pylon-mounted drop tank was also trialled under TG275 of 100- and 200-gallon capacity. These additional cylindrical tanks, regardless of their capacity or shape, seriously affected the longitudinal stability of the Vampire and, as such, the tail structure was subjected to modification. The tailplane chord was increased by 4½in to 46½in, while the elevator chord was reduced by 1½in to 15½in. Large 'acorns' were also fitted where the tail plane and fin joined. The tailplane was also lowered by 13in but still located above the jet efflux and the vertical tail surfaces were redesigned to a more rounded shape reminiscent of the earlier Moth, Rapide and Mosquito.

Powered by a 3,100lb Goblin 2 engine, TG275 was re-designated as the Vampire F.3 on 9 March 1946 but did not make its maiden flight until 4 November 1946. The modifications carried out on TG275 raised the gross weight from 8,578lb to 12,170lb, but the extra fuel capacity saw the fighter's range and endurance almost doubled when a full fuel load was carried.

TG275 was sent to the A&AEE at Boscombe Down in April 1947 for handling trials and clearance for service use. Contracts had already been signed and production orders placed with deliveries commencing from 22 April 1947. In early 1948, the Vampire Trials Unit carried out tests and tropical trials with VG702 and VG703, which were eventually flown back to Britain after carrying out a tour of the Middle East.

Service
In the meantime, 54 Squadron at Odiham, under the command of Sqn Ldr R. W. Oxpring, became the first operational unit to receive the F.3, in April 1948. At the same time, 'rumour control' at Odiham was reporting that the USAF was planning on crossing the Atlantic with its own new F-80 jets, but the Air Ministry had other ideas. Well aware of the long-range capability of the F.3, it was decided that the RAF would cross the Atlantic first and, on 1 July 1948, six Vampires, led by Oxpring, left Odiham for Stornoway. Delayed by strong headwinds, the fighters arrived at Goose Bay on 14 July, and, after carrying out demonstrations across Canada, arrived at Andrews Field, Washington, DC, on 25 July. The Americans had been beaten in becoming the first jet aircraft to cross the Atlantic, because the 56th Fighter Group and 16 F-80 Shooting Stars arrived at Odiham from Selfridge AFB on 21 July.

The Vampire F.3 served with 13 operational RAF squadrons, including six auxiliary squadrons. It was with the latter that the type was retired from the front line in October 1952, when 605 (County of Warwick) Squadron at Honiley re-equipped with the Vampire FB.5. However, the F.3 served on with at least four second line units until March 1954.

Technical Data – DH.100 Vampire F.3	
ENGINE	3,100lb Goblin and Goblin 2
WINGSPAN	40ft
LENGTH	30ft 9in
HEIGHT	8ft 10in
WING AREA	266sq/ft
WEIGHT	7,134lb
ALL-UP WEIGHT	11,970lb
MAX SPEED	531mph
CEILING	43,500ft
RANGE	1,050 miles
ARMAMENT	Four 20mm Hispano Mk V cannons

Vampire F.3 VF345 served de Havilland as a demonstration aircraft in front of representatives from both the Australian and Argentine governments in 1948. Later allocated to 73 Squadron, the Vampire was damaged in a forced landing during a goodwill tour of Italy in September 1949, but was later repaired and sold to the Italian Air Force.

D.H.100 Sea Vampire

Development

The Royal Navy had been very interested in the Vampire ever since the prototype arrived for assessment at the RAE at Farnborough in mid-1944. One of the RAE's tasks was to recommend which aircraft from the batch of early jets on strength, including the E.28/39, Airacomet, Meteor and Vampire, would be most suitable for deck landing trials.

The second prototype Vampire, LZ551/G, had already undergone preliminary modifications with carrier operations in mind. These included larger flaps and dive brakes, which combined to lower the stalling speed and virtually eliminate float. A deck landing assessment was undertaken at Hatfield by the Aerodynamic Flight's commanding officer, Lt Cdr Eric 'Winkle' Brown, who recommended that LZ551/G would be suitable for deck landing trials once an arrestor hook was fitted. The historic event was carried on HMS *Ocean* on 3 December 1946.

Service

Designated as the Sea Vampire F.10, LZ551/G was then passed onto 778 Squadron at Ford, the Service Trials and Carrier Trials Unit, in July 1946 for further evaluation until the aircraft was damaged aboard HMS *Illustrious*. By this time, the Admiralty had already decided that the Sea Vampire would not be suitable for carrier operations because of the engine's slow throttle response and the aircraft's limited range.

On 21 March 1947, an order for 30 Sea Vampire F.20s, serialled VV136 to VV165, was placed. By January 1948, this order had been reduced to just 18 aircraft, serialled VV136 to VV153.

Built at Preston as Vampire FB.5s, all 18 aircraft were flown to Hatfield for conversion to Sea Vampire F.20 standard between November 1947 and January 1948. The prototype F.20 was converted from Vampire F.3 VF317, which arrived at Hatfield on 1 May 1947. Work involved the fitment of a V-frame arrestor hook, which was stored in a small housing above the tail pipe when not deployed. A substantial longer-stroke undercarriage was fitted, which was capable of absorbing a landing of up 16ft/sec. The wings were clipped as per the FB.5 and 'accelerated take-off' hooks were mounted under each wing. The air brakes were increased by 36 per cent over the standard Vampire, as were the split trailing edge flaps, which were 31 per cent larger.

The Sea Vampire F.20 made its service debut with 806 Squadron at RNAS Sydenham when VF315 was delivered by John Cunningham on 20 May 1948. The unit then embarked on HMCS *Magnificent* for a three-month tour of Canada and the US, where the aircraft flew for 40 flying hours and covered 4,000 miles.

Considering how few F.20s were actually built, the aircraft also managed to serve with 700, 728, 759, 764 and 771 Squadrons. The type remained in service until April 1956, when the last examples were retired by 700 Squadron at Ford.

The Sea Vampire T.22 first arrived with the Aircraft Handling Unit (AHU) at Stretton on 18 September 1953 and, after being prepared for service, was allocated to 781 Squadron at Lee-on-Solent from October 1953. 736 Squadron at Lossiemouth and 759 Squadron at Culdrose followed in November 1953, both units conducting operational conversion courses for pilots posted to front-line units. The T.22 saw extensive service with a number of FAA units. The last T.22 in FAA service was XA129, which was operated by the Air Direction School at Yeovilton until July 1970.

Technical Data – Sea Vampire F.20	
ENGINE	3,100lb Goblin 2
WINGSPAN	38ft
LENGTH	30ft 9in
HEIGHT	8ft 10in
WING AREA	262sq/ft
WEIGHT	7,623lb
ALL-UP WEIGHT	12,660lb
MAX SPEED	526mph
CEILING	43,500ft
RANGE	1,140 miles
ARMAMENT	(FB.9) Four 20mm guns and provision for up to 2,000lb of bombs or rockets under the wings

Lt Cdr Brown takes off from the deck of HMS *Ocean* in LZ551/G during the highly successfully trials in early 1946 after the flaps were modified.

Sea Vampire F.20s of 702 Squadron on board HMS *Theseus* on 29 June 1950 during sea trials. Under the command of Lt A. B. B. Clark, VV150 (being manhandled off the carrier's lift in the foreground) was one of six Sea Vampire F.20s allocated to the Naval Jet Evaluation and Training Unit.

De Havilland Sea Vampire F.20 VV149 during an air test out of Hatfield in November 1948. Delivered to 703 Squadron in May 1949, the jet went on to serve with 700, 702 and 771 Squadrons until 1960.

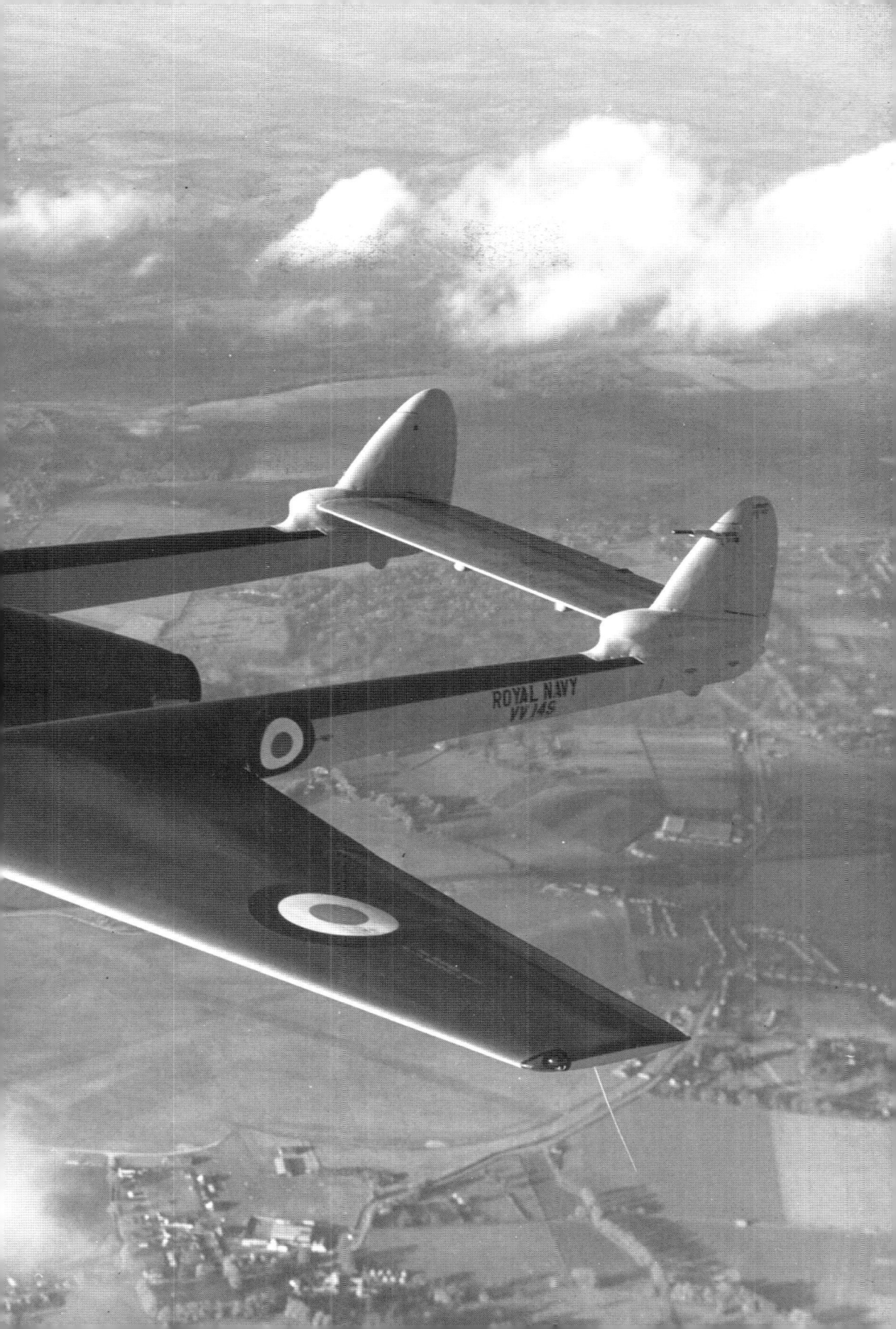

D.H.100 Vampire FB.5 and 9

Development
The Air Ministry was first drawn to idea of a ground-attack Vampire in December 1946 and, not long after, issued Operational Requirement 237 for a ground attack version of the F Mk IV to replace the Tempest.

Design
The Nene-powered Mk IV was destined never to leave the drawing board, but the FB.5, a ground-attack version of the F.3, was. Designed to Specification F.3/47, modifications were to include increased fuel capacity, provision for a pair of 100-gallon drop tanks, a redesigned tailplane and bigger elevator trim tabs. The aircraft also had to be capable of delivering rockets and cannon fire in a dive or at low-level and, finally, the specification called for the FB.5 to be fitted with an ejection seat. The latter request would cause de Havilland many headaches, mainly because the cockpit was only 22in wide and all ejection seats of the day would result in extensive alteration to the fuselage structure. The problem was first looked at in August 1946, when both Malcolm and Martin Baker seats were assessed; neither came close to fitting. While the FB.5 would never be fitted with an ejection seat, the FB.6 (in Swiss service) and the Venom would, thanks to early efforts that had been made to overcome the problem.

Efforts to produce an effective air conditioning system in the Vampire had been going on for quite some time in conjunction with the Institute of Aviation Medicine (IAM) at Farnborough. For the cockpit, an air-conditioning unit, made by George Godfrey and Partners, Ltd of Hanworth, Middlesex, was mounted within the starboard wing root and the FB.9 was born.

Service
The Vampire FB.5 entered service with 16 Squadron at Gütersloh in December 1948. In Germany, the FB.5 would become the backbone of the 2nd Tactical Air Force (TAF), as well as taking over the role of the F.3 within Fighter Command.

The tradition of performing aerobatics with the Vampire was continued with the FB.5 by those units that had formed individual teams, such as 54 Squadron. The squadron demonstrated that the FB.5 was just as good a performer as its predecessor when they put on an amazing display at Farnborough in July 1950 in front of the King and Queen. Not to be outdone, 16 Squadron became the first unit to fly jet fighters that were tied together.

The FB.5 became the first RAF jet fighter to serve in the Far East when 60 Squadron at Tengah re-equipped from the Spitfire FR.18 in December 1950. These aircraft would prove useful in the continuing fight against Communist forces, which had begun in 1948.

In the close-support role, the FB.5 finally relieved the Mosquito of this task, and, at its peak, the definitive RAF Vampire equipped 40 squadrons, including 11 auxiliary squadrons. It was while with the auxiliaries that the type was retired from operational service in March 1957.

In November 1951, the first FB.9s were ferried to the Mediterranean to re-equip 73 Squadron at Ta Kali, Malta, which was operating the FB.5. From early 1952, FB.9s began to be ferried in large numbers by Transport Command pilots to units in the Middle and Far East. On their return, the unit's FB.5s were flown back to Britain to serve on in a secondary role. The last single-seater variant of the Vampire to enter RAF service, the FB.9 served with 18 operational squadrons until the type was retired in March 1957 with the disbandment of 613 and 614 Squadrons.

Technical Data – Vampire FB.5	
ENGINE	3,100lb Goblin 2
WINGSPAN	38ft
LENGTH	30ft 9in
HEIGHT	8ft 10in
WING AREA	262sq/ft
WEIGHT	7,253lb
ALL-UP WEIGHT	12,360lb
MAX SPEED	535mph
CEILING	40,000ft
RANGE	1,145 miles
ARMAMENT	(FB.9) Four 20mm guns and provision for up to 2,000lb of bombs or rockets under the wings

Right: The RAF College at RAF Cranwell flew all marks of Vampire from the F.3 until the mid-1960s, including this quartet of FB.9s.

Below: A trio of Vampire FB.5s serving with 102 Flying Refresher School out of North Luffenham, which only existed from April to November 1951.

Vampire FB.9s, WL559 'P', WR236 and WL586 of 8 Squadron over Aden in 1953.

D.H.100 Vampire (Export Variants)

Available in a variety of export versions, the Vampire was a cost-effective piece of military hardware that helped many of the world's air forces to enter the jet era with little fuss. The first of them was the FB.6, which was designed as a single-seat fighter-bomber, an aircraft that came about because of international interest shown in the FB.5. The Swiss government placed an order for 75 aircraft powered by the Goblin, which, following trials in June 1947, were designated as the FB.6 in August. Later built under licence in Switzerland, orders were also placed by the Swedish, who designated the aircraft as the FB.50 and, in service, the J.28B. Twelve FB.6s were converted into target presentation aircraft in 1978 and featured a Venom-style nose. The main export version of the FB.6 was the FB.52.

The Vampire FB.25 was the export variant of the FB.5, of which only 25 were exported to New Zealand. The first Vampires to be built in Australia were the Nene-powered F.30. John 'Blackjack' Walker carried out the maiden flight on 29 June 1949. The first 57 of 80 built featured the same 'elephant's ear' intakes on the upper fuselage as the F.2 but, following issues with high-speed handling, these were repositioned to the lower fuselage. The remaining 23 of this batch were built as FB.31s. The Australian-built Nene-powered FB.31 featured stronger wings with squared off tips, which were very similar to the FB.5. Only one aircraft was converted to FB.32 standard, which had larger intakes, an ejection seat and an air-conditioned cockpit. Powered by a Goblin 35, the Australians produced three different trainer variants (beginning with the T.33), which were constructed to the same specification as the RAF's T.11. The T.34 followed, of which only five were built to the same standard as the early Sea Vampire T.22 to train crews for the Sea Venom. Upgraded at a later date, these five aircraft were re-designated as T.34As. The T.35 was similar to the T.33/34 family but was constructed to the same specification as the later production RAF T.11s, complete with one-piece canopies and ejection seats. Several T.33s were converted to this specification and these aircraft were given the designation T.35A.

Built under licence by Sud-Est, the FB.51 was effectively an FB.5 that was assembled in France with British components. The first of 67 Goblin-powered Vampires, which were supplied in component form, made its maiden flight from Marignane on 27 January 1950.

The main export version of the FB.6 was the successful FB.52, of which 193 were sold to ten countries, between December 1949 and October 1953. In addition, 353 FB.52s were built under licence in Italy and India and further FB.52As were supplied to the Italian Air Force from Chester between July 1950 and December 1951. Twenty-seven FB.52As were also licence-built by the Macchi Company in Italy.

The export version of the Vampire NF.10 was the NF.54, of which 14 'new build' aircraft were sold to Italy between 1951 and 1953. The designation was also applied to 30 ex-RAF NF.10s, which were refurbished for the Indian Air Force and delivered between 1954 and 1958.

Vampire T.55

The export version of the DH.115 Trainer, the T.55 was another success story, over 200 were built from scratch and a further half dozen were converted from T.11s. The T.55 was also built under licence in Switzerland and India, the latter converted several of its aircraft to PR.55 standard.

D.H 100 Vampire (Export Variants)

Technical Data – Vampire FB.52 and FB.52A	
ENGINE	3,350lb Goblin 3
WINGSPAN	38ft
LENGTH	30ft 9in
HEIGHT	8ft 10in
WING AREA	262sq/ft
WEIGHT	7,283lb
ALL-UP WEIGHT	12,360lb
MAX SPEED	548mph
CEILING	42,800ft
RANGE	1,220 miles
ARMAMENT	Four 20mm guns and provision for up to 2,000lb of bombs or rockets under the wings

Right: This aircraft, Vampire T.55 '333', together with six Vampire FB.52s, formed the Iraqi Air Force's first jet fighter unit, 5 Squadron based at El-Rashid, near Baghdad.

Below: Federal Works (F+W)-built Vampire FB.6s, J-1170 and J-1192; two of 100 built under licence between 1950 and 1952. The duo is pictured in the early 1980s, when several surviving FB.6s were updated with new UHF radio equipment which was fitted into a Venom-type upturned nose.

D.H.103 Hornet F Mk 1 to 4

Development
A slightly smaller version of the Mosquito, the D.H.103 Hornet was designed specifically as a long-range fighter capable of island-hopping during the final push against the Japanese in the Pacific theatre. However, the war in the Far East was over by the time that the Hornet had entered service, and the full potential of this potent aircraft was never realised.

Design
Just like the Mosquito before it, work began on the Hornet as a private venture, and it was only at a later stage that Specification F.12/43 was written around it. The aircraft used the same ply/balsa/ply method of construction for the fuselage as the Mosquito, while a new composite wood and metal wing was fitted. Power was provided by a pair of Merlin 130/131 engines with a reduced frontal area, each driving a de Havilland Hydromatic propeller, both of which rotated towards the fuselage to reduce the tendency to swing on take-off.

The Hornet was built in four production variants beginning with the initial F Mk 1, followed by the PR Mk 2, which was a conversion of the F Mk I with cameras mounted in the rear fuselage. The F Mk 3 was the most common variant, and the aircraft featured a dorsal fillet (retrofitted to all variants), greater fuel capacity and more hard-points under the wings for a variety of stores. The FR Mk 4 were late production F Mk 3s, which had the rear fuel tank removed to be replaced with a camera.

Service
The prototype Hornet, RR915, made its maiden flight on 28 July 1944, and deliveries to the RAF began in April 1945. The first F Mk 1s did not join 64 Squadron at Horsham St Faith until May 1946, followed by 19 Squadron at Church Fenton in October. The Hornet was the fastest piston-engined fighter to be flown operationally by the RAF. Initially introduced into the interceptor role, this was changed to that of a low-level day intruder from 1949, because manoeuvrability had been found to be lacking at altitude.

The type saw action as part of the Far East Air Force (FEAF) with 33 Squadron; the unit carried out innumerable successful rocket strikes in Malaya. The Brigands of 45 Squadron were replaced by Hornets in the same role, one that the twin-engined fighter proved to be particularly successful at. The last Hornets were withdrawn from 45 Squadron in June 1955 to be replaced by the Vampire. The aircraft was the last piston-engined fighter to serve the RAF operationally.

Production
Total production of the Hornet amounted to 206 aircraft, comprising two prototypes; 60 F Mk 1s; five PR Mk 2s converted from F Mk 1s; 132 F Mk 3s; and a dozen FR Mk 4 conversions from F Mk 3 airframes.

Technical Data – DH.103 Hornet F Mk 3

ENGINE	Two 2,070hp Rolls-Royce Merlin 130/13
WINGSPAN	45ft
LENGTH	36ft 8in
HEIGHT	14ft 2in
WING AREA	361sq/ft
EMPTY WEIGHT	12,880lb
LOADED WEIGHT	20,900lb
MAX SPEED	427mph at 22,000ft
INITIAL CLIMB	4,000ft/min
SERVICE CEILING	35,000ft
RANGE	3,000 miles
ARMAMENT	Four 20mm guns in nose and provision for 2,000lb of bombs or rockets

Right: De Havilland D.H.103 Hornet F Mk 1 PX244 captured during a pre-delivery test flight out of Hatfield. The aircraft went to serve with 65 Squadron and 41 Squadron but was wrecked in a forced landing after both engines cut six miles northwest of Derby on 4 November 1948.

Below: Hornet F Mk 3s of 64 Squadron at Linton on Ouse in May 1948. PX345 in the foreground later joined 80 Squadron until it was SOC on 6 May 1955.

D.H.103 Sea Hornet F Mk 20, NF Mk 21 and PR Mk 22

Development
The basic requirements for an aircraft operating from a carrier were good low-speed handling and excellent visibility for the pilot; the Hornet ticked both boxes. Not long after the Hornet flew, Specification N.5/44 was issued in advance of the modifications needed to navalise the aircraft into the Sea Hornet.

Design
Three aircraft, PX212, PX214 and PX219, were all built as Hornet F Mk 1s, but were taken from the production line for conversion into the Sea Hornet prototypes. The task of carrying out the conversion work was entrusted to the Heston Aircraft Co. Ltd. The work involved fitment of a new Lockheed hydraulically powered folding wing, like the Sea Mosquito, a forged steel arrestor hook and the necessary mounts for a Naval radar system and radio equipment. De Havilland produced a more substantial Airdraulic undercarriage, which could take the punishment of the high rate of descent required for deck landings.

Three variants were built: the standard fully navalised F.20, the two-seat NF Mk 21 night fighter with non-folding wings, ASH radar and flame-damped exhausts, and the PR Mk 22, which was similar to the F Mk 20 but was fitted with a pair of F.52 cameras and a single Fairchild K.16B camera.

Service
The first of three Sea Hornet prototypes, PX212, made its maiden flight on 19 April 1945; the aircraft at this stage was merely a hooked Hornet. PX919 was the first fully navalised version c, and this commenced carrier trails on HMS *Ocean* on 10 August, before joining 703 Squadron for service trials. The F Mk 20 entered service with 801 Squadron at Ford on 1 June 1947, and remained in FAA service until 1951 but continued on in the second line with 723 Squadron at Half Far until 1955.

The NF Mk 21 first flew on 9 July 1946 and, after trials with the Service Trials Unit and the Naval Air Fighting Development Unit, the type entered service with 809 Squadron at Culdrose on 20 January 1949. The NF Mk 21 was relegated to the second line in 1954 but, within two years, the majority were scrapped at Yeovilton.

Basically a navalised version of the RAF's PR Mk 2, the Sea Hornet PR Mk 2 made its public appearance at the 1948 SBAC at Farnborough. The aircraft went to serve with 703, 738, 739, 759, 878, 801, 809 and 1833 Squadrons.

Production
In total, 203 Sea Hornets were built, comprising three prototypes, 78 F Mk 20s, 79 NF Mk 21s and 43 PR Mk 22s between 1945 and 12 June 1951.

Technical Data – DH.103 Sea Hornet NF Mk 21	
ENGINE	Two 2,030hp Rolls-Royce Merlin 133/134
WINGSPAN	45ft
LENGTH	37ft
HEIGHT	13ft
WING AREA	361sq/ft
EMPTY WEIGHT	14,230lb
ALL-UP WEIGHT	19,530lb
MAX SPEED	430mph at 22,000ft
INITIAL CLIMB	4,400ft/min
SERVICE CEILING	36,500ft
RANGE	1,500 miles
ARMAMENT	Four 20mm guns in nose and provision for 2,000lb of bombs or eight 60lb rockets

De Havilland D.H.103 Sea Hornet F Mk 20 TT202 spent much of its service live carrying out trials with the A&AEE, RAE and 703 Squadron.

Sea Hornet F Mk 20 TT198 'F' during RP trials with 703 Squadron operating out of Thorney Island.

A line of 809 Squadron NF Mk 21s enjoying some shore on Gibraltar in the early 1950s. The unit operated all three marks of Sea Hornet between January 1949 and May 1952.

D.H.104 Devon C Mk 1, 2 and Sea Devon Mk 20

Development
The D.H.104 Dove family of aircraft came about as a post-war replacement for the D.H.89 Dragon Rapide. Designed by R. E. Bishop in 1944, the prototype Dove made its maiden flight on 25 September 1945, and, within a few years, captured the attention of the military.

Design
A low wing monoplane, the D.H.104 was an attractive-looking twin-engined, all-metal aircraft, with the exception of the elevators and rudder, which were fabric-covered. The Gipsy Queen engines were fitted with reversible-pitch propellers, the first British transport aircraft to make use of this form of braking assistance.

To de Havilland, the military variants of the D.H.104 were the Dove 4, and in military service, they were called the Devon. Designed to Specification C.13/46, the C Mk 1 version only differed from a standard Dove in having a reduced capacity of two crew and seven passengers, as the forward starboard seat was replaced by a J Type dinghy. The aircraft that would serve the Royal Navy were called the Sea Devon C.20; the majority of them were ex-civilian machines without any specialist modifications.

Eight RAF C Mk 1s were fitted with Gipsy Queen 175 engines in 1965 by Hawker Siddeley and Maintenance Units (MUs). These aircraft were all later fitted with a raised Dove 8 type canopy and these modifications would later form the basis of the C Mk 2 conversion; 28 C Mk 1s were converted to C Mk 2 standard.

Service
The first examples of the Devon C Mk 1 were delivered in 1947 and were allocated to 31 (Metropolitan Communications) Squadron, Hendon, in January 1949 and served the unit until March 1955. All 30 aircraft delivered were employed in a wide range of units and, following conversion to C Mk 2 standard, a number were allocated to squadrons in the late 1960s. 21, 26 and 207 Squadrons, all reformed in February 1969, were allocated the Devon C Mk 2 and, following the disbandment of 21 and 26 Squadrons in 1976, only 207 Squadron operated the type until it was finally retired in June 1984.

The Sea Devon C.20 began to arrive in 1955 and was first allocated to 781 Squadron in April, followed by 765 Squadron in February 1957, 750 Squadron in March and 771 Squadron in January 1983. It was the latter unit that was the last bastion of the Sea Devon, its service coming to an end in December 1989.

Production
The Air Ministry originally placed an order for 50 Devon C Mk 1s, which was later reduced to 30 aircraft, built to Contract 6/ACFT/235 and delivered between October 1947 and June 1949. This batch was serialled VP952 to VP981. A further group of six C Mk 1s were added, serialled WB530 to WB535, WF984, XA879, XA880 and XG496 (ex-G-ANDX). C Mk 2 conversions were VP952, VP953, VP955, VP956, VP957-963, VP965, VP967 (later loaned to the FAA), VP968, VP971, VP973-978, VP981, WB530, WB531, WB533, WB534, WB535, XA880. Ten Sea Devon C Mk 20s were serialled XJ319 to XJ324 and XJ347 to XJ350, XK895 to XK897.

D.H.104 Devon C Mk 1, 2 and Sea Devon Mk 20

Technical Data – DH.104 Devon C Mk 1 and 2	
ENGINE	(1) Two 330hp de Havilland Gipsy Queen 71 or 340hp Gipsy Queen 70-4; (2) two 400 Gipsy Queen 175; (Sea Devon) two 340hp Gipsy Queen 70-4
WINGSPAN	57ft
LENGTH	39ft 4in
HEIGHT	13ft 4in
WING AREA	335sq/ft
EMPTY WEIGHT	5,560lb
ALL-UP WEIGHT	8,500lb
MAX SPEED	201mph
INITIAL CLIMB	850ft/min
SERVICE CEILING	20,000ft
RANGE	1,000 miles

Right: **Devon C Mk 1 VP968 in service with the Fighter Command Communications Squadron in the 1950s. The aircraft was later upgraded to C.2 standard and served out its final military days with 207 Squadron, Northolt.**

Below: **Originally laid down as a Dove 2, XJ347 was taken on charge by the Royal Navy in September 1954. The aircraft remained in military hands until 1982 and was registered as G-AXMT, its original registration dating back to 1953. After 8619.20 flying hours, the aircraft was grounded in the late 1990s.**

D.H.106 Comet C Mk 2, T Mk 2 and R Mk 2

Development
The world's first jet-powered airliner to enter commercial service, the Comet would always be a ground-breaking aircraft, despite the setbacks that had befallen it. In the form of the improved Series 2, the Comet would also become the first jet-powered airliner to serve the RAF.

Design
The RAF ordered three different variants of the Comet, the main one being the pure transport C Mk 2. They differed from the earlier Comet 1s by having Avon rather than Ghost engines and, specific to the military, the freight doors were strengthened. Two aircraft were designated as T Mk 2s for crew training duties, while three were built as the R Mk 2 (aka C Mk 2 RCM or C(RCM)2). The latter were built for 'special duties' with 90 (Signals) Group, which specialised in electronic intelligence (ELINT) operations.

Service
The first Comet for the RAF was the first of two T Mk 2 trainers delivered to 216 Squadron at Lyneham in July 1956. A further eight Comet C Mk 2s joined 216 Squadron, while the first of three R Mk 2s was delivered to 192 Squadron at Wyton in July 1957. 192 Squadron was renumbered as 51 Squadron at Watton in August 1958, by which time, three R Mk 2s were on strength and a fourth and fifth, ex-C Mk 2s XK655 and XK695, were being converted. Three more C Mk 2s would be allocated to the squadron for crew training until the type was withdrawn in the mid-1970s.

216 Squadron, which had become the world's first jet transport squadron, began operations on 23 June 1956, when it transported the Minister for Air to Moscow for Soviet Air Force Day. From late 1959 onwards, each of 216 Squadron's Comets were given names, starting with XK669 (*Taurus*), XK670 (*Corvus*), XK671 (*Aquila*), XK695 (*Perseus*), XK696 (*Orion*), XK697 (*Cygnus*), XK698 (*Pegasus*), XK699 (*Sagittarius*), XK715 (*Columbo*), and XK716 (*Cepheus*). The capability of Transport Command was transformed overnight by the far-reaching Comet C Mk 2s, which remained in service until April 1967. In the ELINT role, the R Mk 2s were retained by 51 Squadron until January 1975 when the Nimrod R Mk 1, which had arrived in July 1971, finally took over.

Production
Thirteen Series 2 Comets were delivered to the RAF between June 1956 and February 1958 to Contract 6/ACFT/11808 (first three aircraft built as R Mk 2s) and 6/ACFT/11809. Aircraft were three R Mk 2s (XK655, XK659 and XK663), a pair of T Mk 2s (XK669 to XK670) and the remainder as new build C Mk 2s (XK671, XK695 to XK699, XK815 and XK716).

The RAF also took delivery of the following Comets: 1XB XM823 and XM829; Comet 2E XN453, which served with the A&AEE and RAE until 197; Comet 3B XP915 for service with BLEU until the early 1970s; and Comet 2E XV144 (G-AMXK) for MinTech/BLEU.

Technical Data – DH.106 Comet C MK 2	
ENGINE	Four 7,300lb st Rolls-Royce Avon 117
WINGSPAN	115ft
LENGTH	96ft
HEIGHT	28ft 4½in
WING AREA	2,027sq/ft
EMPTY WEIGHT	53,870lb
ALL-UP WEIGHT	120,000lb
MAX CRUISING SPEED	480mph at 38,000ft
MAX RANGE	2,200 miles
ACCOMMODATION	Five crew and 44 passengers

Comet C Mk 2 XK698, named *Pegasus*, spent its entire career with 216 Squadron operating from Lyneham.

To all the thousands of servicemen who passed through Lyneham over the past 30 years, the impressive sight of C Mk 2 XK669 *Sagittarius* (nicknamed 'Saggie') on the gate was hard to miss. The last example of the C Mk 2 family, this aircraft was butchered in November 2013 and only the forward fuselage survived at Old Sarum.

D.H.106 Comet C Mk 4

Development
The Comet 4 represented the definitive version of de Havilland's jet airliner, aided by engines that had twice the power of the original Ghosts. Over 18ft longer than the Comet 1, the Series 4 could carry up to 119 passengers and, thanks to the extended fuselage and pinion tanks on the wings, range was significantly improved.

The Comet 4 was an excellent aircraft, giving good service all over the world. The last of the 4s were delivered in 1964. BOAC retired its Comet 4 fleet the following year, but the type remained commonplace until 1981 when the last examples were retired by Dan-Air.

Design
It was during the 1961 SBAC at Farnborough that the military first showed an interest in de Havilland's latest Comet, the 4C. It was at the event that the RAF placed an order for five aircraft, to be designated C Mk 4. The cabin was configured for 94 passengers in rearward-facing seats but could also be quickly converted into an air ambulance for a dozen stretcher cases, 47 sitting cases and six sick berth attendants.

Service
Serialled XR395 to XR399, the first aircraft made its maiden flight from Chester to Hatfield on 15 November 1961. Delivered to 216 Squadron from December 1961, the first aircraft, XR395, spent some time with the A&AEE at Boscombe Down before joining its colleagues at Lyneham.

The Comet C Mk 4s, operating alongside the C Mk 2s (until April 1967), contributed greatly to extending the capability of Transport Command and, despite only a comparative handful being in service, there were not many RAF stations across the globe that the C Mk 4s would not regularly appear at. In the swinging defence cuts of 1975, the Comet C Mk 4s were some of the many victims, but their usefulness was far from over. All five were sold on 1 September 1975 to Dan-Air as G-BDIT, 'U, 'V, 'W and 'X and remained in service until late 1980/early 1981, flying the last commercial Comet flights. G-BDIU (ex-XR396) gave further service to the military when it was flown to British Aerospace, Bitteswell, on 9 July 1981 where the airframe contributed to the Nimrod airborne early warning (AEW) programme.

Production
There was an initial order for five Comet C Mk 4s, delivered between December 1961 and February 1962 by de Havilland, Chester, to Contract KD/G/054 and serialled XR395 to XR399. Four other Comets from the Series 4 family saw service in military markings. These were Comet 4C XS235 *Canopus*, Comet 4 XV814 (ex-G-APDF), Comet 4 XW626 (ex-G-APDS [Nimrod AEW trials]), and Comet 4 XX944 (ex-G-APDP [AEW test bed]).

D.H.106 Comet C Mk 4

Technical Data – DH.106 Comet C Mk 4	
ENGINE	Four 10,500lb st Rolls-Royce Avon 350
WINGSPAN	114ft 10in
LENGTH	118ft
HEIGHT	28ft 6in
WING AREA	2,121sq/ft
ALL-UP WEIGHT	162,000lb
CRUISING SPEED	503mph
MAX RANGE	2,650 miles
PASSENGERS	94

Right: **The difference in size between the Comet C Mk 2 and the C Mk 4 is graphically illustrated in this rare 216 Squadron two-ship.**

Below: **Comet 4C XW626 (ex-G-APDS) was converted and used as a Nimrod airborne early warning development aircraft, hence the large forward radome. The Comet was scrapped at Bedford in 1994.**

D.H.108 Swallow

Development
The design work of the DH.108 was already at an advanced stage when the project was given some weight by the Air Ministry, which issued Specification E.1/45 (OR.195) for a pair of experimental tailless research aircraft in support of the DH.106 Comet. The remit was later fine-tuned to Specification E.11/45, still for two aircraft but one was to be built to explore low-speed handling and the other to test the high-speed handling of the swept wing.

Design
Ordered under Contract SB.66562, dated 13 December 1945, the two prototype DH.108s, unofficially named 'Swallow', were to be serialled VN856 and VN860. Instead, a pair of Vampire F Mk 1 fuselages, serialled TG283 and TG306, were taken off the production line and serials VN856 and VN860 were cancelled.

TG283 would be the first prototype, and as such was designed for low-speed handling. The original Vampire fuselage was lengthened and covered in light alloy. The aircraft had a pair of all-metal wings with a 43° sweep, complete with a set of Handley Page slats on the outer leading edge of the wing, locked in the open position restricting the top speed to 280mph. A conventional swept single fin and rudder was fitted at the rear of the fuselage while elevons were fitted to the trailing edge of the outer wing and large split trailing edge flaps were mounted inboard.

Service
TG283 was taken by road to Woodbridge on 5 May 1946. With Geoffrey de Havilland, Jr at the controls, a high-speed taxi run on 11 May turned into a quick hop, prior to the DH.108 making its maiden flight on 15 May 1946.

The second DH.108, TG306, designed to evaluate the high-speed characteristics of the swept wing, differed from the first aircraft in several ways. TG306 made its maiden flight, once again in the hands of de Havilland, Jr from Hatfield on 23 August 1946. On 27 September, de Havilland, Jr took off at 1730hrs in TG306 from Hatfield for a simulated record attempt after a high Mach 0.87 (662mph) run was performed over Thames Estuary. On reaching 10,000ft, TG306 was entered into a dive to investigate controllability. At approximately 5,000ft, the aircraft suffered a violent structural failure and disintegration. It is believed that at one point the aircraft had reached Mach 0.90 (685mph) before both wings failed at their root-end attachment points, forcing them to fold rearwards. Geoffrey de Havilland Jr, OBE, was killed instantly.

Sir Geoffrey de Havilland announced in November 1946 that research work with the DH.108 would continue. The modified third prototype, VW120, made its maiden flight from Hatfield in the hands of John Cunningham on 24 July 1947.

The performance of VW120 was encouraging, so it was decided to have a crack at the FAI Class C.1/1 100km record, which, by April 1948, was held by Mike Lithgow in the Attacker at 564.88mph. On 12 April, John Derry took off in VW120 in an attempt to break the record, which he smashed with a speed of 605.23mph. Derry continued to raise the bar in VW120, becoming the first British pilot to exceed Mach 1.0 on 6 September 1948.

After being transferred to the RAE, TG283 was lost on 1 May 1950 during trials with Sqn Ldr G. E. C. Genders at the controls; the aircraft crashed near Hartley Wintney, Hampshire.

VW120 concluded its flight trials on 28 June 1949, and was handed over to the RAE to carry out high-speed longitudinal stability and aero-elastic distortion at high Mach number trials. It was during one of the latter that VW120 was lost with Sqn Ldr J. S. R. Muller-Rowland at the controls on 15 February 1950. So came to an end a period of British flight testing, which contributed a great deal to the development of the swept wing but at the price of three pilots' lives. Between May 1946 and May 1950, the three Swallows had accumulated 480 test flights and a plethora of technical data and knowledge that would be put to good use in the future.

Technical Data – D.H.108 Swallow	
ENGINE	(TG283) One 3,000lb st de Havilland Goblin 2; (TG306) One 3,300lb Goblin 3; (VW120) One 3,750lb Goblin 4
WINGSPAN	39ft
LENGTH	(TG283) 25ft 10in; (TG306) 24ft 6in; (VW120) 26ft 9½in
WING AREA	328sq/ft
ALL-UP WEIGHT	(TG283) 8,800lb; (TG306) 8,960lb
MAX SPEED	(TG283) 280mph; (TG306) 640mph

Right: The second DH.108, TG306, with Geoffrey de Havilland at the controls not long after its maiden flight in August 1946.

Below: De Havilland DH.108 VW120, the third prototype, joined by Vampire F.1 TG278.

DH.108 VW120 pictured after transfer to the RAE in July 1949, where it would carry out high-speed trials until its loss on 15 February 1950.

D.H.110 and Sea Vixen FAW Mk 1

Development
The last, and by far the largest, development of the original Vampire/Venom family of aircraft, the D.H.110 was first proposed in 1946. Designed from the outset as a naval all-weather fighter, the aircraft was modified in 1948 to compete for an Air Ministry specification for a two-seat transonic fighter for the RAF, which would ultimately be the Gloster Javelin. Two prototypes were ordered and built at Hatfield under the leadership of J. P. Smith.

Design
The D.H.110 was an impressive-looking machine with an all-metal, stressed structure with twin-booms and a swept wing that owed much to the efforts of the D.H.108 for its design. The aircraft was installed with powered controls, armed with a pair of 30mm Aden cannon and powered by two Rolls-Royce engines, positioned side by side, to the rear of the fuselage.

When the RAF chose the Javelin instead of the D.H.110 and the Royal Navy lost interest in the D.H.116 (modernised Venom), the senior service turned towards the big de Havilland twin-boom fighter. Once fully navalised with power-folding wings, a hinged and pointed radome, long stroke undercarriage, arrestor hook and the Aden guns removed, the aircraft re-appeared as the Sea Venom Mk 20X.

Service
The first of three prototypes was D.H.110 WG236, which was first flown by John Cunningham on 26 September 1951. It was this aircraft that tragically crashed at the SBAC on 6 September 1952, killing John Derry, Tony Richards and 31 spectators on the ground. The second prototype, WG240, first flew on 25 July 1952, and following the crash was not back in the air until June 1954, following multiple modifications. The third prototype was the semi-navalised XF628, the Sea Vixen Mk 20X, which first flew from Christchurch on 20 June 1955. XF628 carried out the first arrested deck landing on HMS *Ark Royal* on 6 April 1956.

The first production aircraft designated Sea Vixen FAW Mk 1 was XJ474 and first flew from Christchurch on 20 March 1957. Following extensive trials at Boscombe Down and with HMS *Ark Royal* and *Centaur*, the Sea Vixen was cleared for service. The FAW Mk 1 entered service with 'Y' Flight of 700 Squadron in November 1958 and, after further trials with HMS *Victorious*, the first operational Sea Vixen unit was formed in the shape of 892 Squadron at Yeovilton, which joined HMS *Ark Royal* in February 1960.

The FAW Mk 1 also served with 766, 890, 893 and 899 Squadrons before it began to be replaced by the FAW Mk 2 from 1966 onwards. One FAW Mk 1, XJ481, escaped conversion and was used by the A&AEE at Boscombe Down until 1974, when it was donated to the FAA Museum at Yeovilton.

Production
A total of 114 Sea Vixen FAW Mk 1s were built between 1957 and 1963, serialled XJ474 to XJ494, XJ513 to XJ528, XJ556 to XJ586, XJ602 to XJ611, XN647 to XN658, XN683 to XN710 and XP918.

Technical Data – DH.110 and Sea Vixen FAW Mk 1	
ENGINE	(110) Two Rolls-Royce Avons; (FAW Mk 1) Two 10,000lb st Rolls Royce Avon 208s
WINGSPAN	50ft
LENGTH	(110) 52ft 1½in; (FAW Mk 1) 55ft 7in
HEIGHT	10ft 9in
WING AREA	648sq/ft
ALL-UP WEIGHT	(FAW Mk 1) 35,000lb
MAX SPEED	(FAW Mk 1) 645mph at 10,000ft
CLIMB RATE	(FAW Mk 1) 6½ mins to 40,000ft
CEILING	(FAW Mk 1) 48,000ft
ARMAMENT	Four de Havilland Firestreak missiles, two Microcell unguided 2in rocket packs, and four 500lb or two 1,000lb bombs

Right: The second prototype de Havilland D.H.110, WG240, first flew on 25 July 1952. It would take a decade of intense development before this machine evolved in the operational Sea Vixen FAW Mk 1.

Below: A line of FAW Mk 1s belonging to reformed 892 Squadron at Yeovilton in 1959, the first operational unit to receive the type. The squadron re-equipped with the FAW Mk 2 in December 1965.

D.H.110 Sea Vixen FAW Mk 2

Development
Despite the ten years of development that it took to get the Sea Vixen FAW Mk 1 into service, there was still room for further improvements, which resulted in the last of the twin-boom fighters, the FAW Mk 2.

Design
The FAW Mk 2 featured a number of modifications, which included the ability to carry the same Firestreak missiles as the FAW Mk 1 or four Red air-to-air missiles or the new air-to-ground Bullpup missile. The only most obvious external change between the two variants was the extension of the tail booms over the leading edge of the wing, which was filled with extra fuel tanks, thus extending the aircraft's range. The extension changed the aerodynamics of the wing, which meant that the 1,000lb bomb could no longer be carried. The method of escape from the FAW Mk 2 was improved and additional ECM equipment was installed.

Service
A pair of FAW Mk 1s were used as the development aircraft for the new variant, and the two aircraft made their maiden flights on 1 June and 17 August 1962, respectively. Both were later brought up to full FAW Mk 2 standard, followed by 14 Mk 1s, which were completed at Chester as Mk 2s; the first of the latter flew on 8 March 1963.

The first FAW Mk 2 to enter operational service joined 899 Squadron in February 1964; the aircraft later embarking on HMS *Eagle* bound for the Far East. Operational training on the FAW Mk 2 was provided by 766 Squadron (Naval Air Fighter School) at Yeovilton, which had already made a name for itself with its FAW Mk 1 display team, 'Fred's Five'. The unit received its first FAW Mk 2, XS582, on 7 July 1965.

The FAW Mk 2 proved to be a very useful aerial tanker, which was put to the test during exercises off Cyprus in 1967, when aircraft from 892 Squadron, HMS *Hermes*, refuelled Lightnings of 56 Squadron. 892 Squadron also had a display team of its own called 'Simon's Sircus', which gave several breath-taking performances at the 1968 SBAC. The same year, 893 Squadron carried out a record-breaking long distance flight, for an FAA unit, by flying from Yeovilton to Akrotiri, a distance of 2,200 miles, refuelled along the way by RAF Victors.

The operational withdrawal of the FAW Mk 2 began in 1972 and started HMS *Eagle* being decommissioned. Aircraft from 891 Squadron were already being transferred to the FRU, which was operated by Airwork Ltd at Yeovilton from 1971, and, in 1974, the remaining examples were transferred to Flight Refuelling Ltd. It was the latter company that converted a number of FAW Mk 2s to D.3 drone standard and at least three pilotless Sea Vixens were tested at RAE Llanbedr before the idea was abandoned. Later used as targets, these aircraft were not retired until 1984.

Production
FAW Mk 2 production comprised a pair of FAW Mk 1s converted as development aircraft; 14 FAW MK 2s converted to FAW Mk 2 standard before they left the factory; 15 new build aircraft; and 67 conversions of FAW Mk 1s already in service to FAW Mk 2 standard.

D.H.110 Sea Vixen FAW Mk 2

Technical Data – DH.110 Sea Vixen FAW Mk 2	
ENGINE	Two 10,000lb st Rolls Royce Avon 208s
WINGSPAN	50ft
LENGTH	55ft 7in
HEIGHT	10ft 9in
WING AREA	648sq/ft
ALL-UP WEIGHT	37,000lb
MAX SPEED	640mph at 10,000ft
CLIMB RATE	8½ mins to 40,000ft
CEILING	48,000ft
ARMAMENT	Four Red Top air-to-air missiles or four Bullpup air-to-surface missiles, two Microcell unguided 2in rocket packs, and four 500lb bombs

Right: Originally built as an FAW Mk 1, XN684 is pictured as a part-converted 'interim' FAW Mk 2 for trials with the Red Top air-to-air missile.

Below: First flown from Christchurch as an FAW Mk 1 on 23 March 1961, XN653 was modified to FAW Mk 2 standard in 1964. The aircraft is pictured in service with 899 Squadron, coded '313/H', at Yeovilton in 1966.

D.H.112 Venom FB.1 and 4

Development

In early 1950, full production of the Venom was authorised, and exciting plans were made for the Venom, along with the Republic F-84, to become a standard NATO fighter-bomber. A scheme was drawn up at the Palais de Chaillot for over 2,000 Venoms to be built, with 1,185 being produced in the UK by de Havilland, Bristol and Fairey. On the continent, assembly centres were to be established by Macchi and Fiat in Italy (as the Fiat G.81) and Sud-Aviation in France, which was already building the Vampire as the SE.535 Mistral. Unfortunately, this ambitious idea, which would have seen the Venom become as common a sight in European skies as the F-84, never came to fruition, thanks to the debilitating decline in the British aviation industry at the time.

Service

Orders for the RAF were drastically cut back but eventually 375 Venom FB.1s (serialled WE255–WE483, WK389–WK503 and WR272–WR373) entered service; the first with 11 Squadron at Wünstorf in August 1952 as part of the 2nd TAF. The new jet was initially received with enthusiasm by RAF pilots but, after a few aircraft were lost to structural failure, some doubts began to creep in. A stringent +2g manoeuvre limitation was imposed and the lack of an ejection seat and air conditioning saw the Venom's honeymoon period come to an abrupt end. The aircraft's poor roll rate was also criticised but, on the whole, the Venom was an equal to the straight-wing F-84 at all heights and was on a par with the Ouragan. However, when it came to taking on a Canberra, the Venom failed to get anywhere near, and the F-86 was in a different league.

The Venom FB.1 served with several squadrons in West Germany, the Middle East and Far East and, after the initial limitations were removed, was accepted with muted praise by many service pilots. But the lack of ejection seats, accompanied by a steady flow of accidents, many resulting from further structural failures, forced de Havilland to consider developing the Venom still further. Thus, the FB.4 was born when a modified FB.1, WE381, was first flown on 29 December 1953.

The FB.4 was an attempt to rectify all of the original mark's serious deficiencies, starting with the fitment of a Martin Baker Mk I ejection seat and a Godfrey air-conditioning system. A descent rate of roll was introduced by installing a set of hydraulically boosted ailerons and the rudders were also powered. The tail was aerodynamically improved with front and rear facing bullets and the fins and rudders were also enlarged. The FB.4 was a considerably more purposeful aircraft, but by then it was the mid-1950s, and the Venom had sadly missed its chance as slippery jets like the Hunter were leading the field.

The first of 150 FB.4s (serialled WR374–WR564) entered service in 1955 and, along with the Hunter, quickly replaced the FB.1 in Europe, the Middle and Far East. The FB.4 went on to see a great deal of action in Aden, Cyprus, Malaya, Oman and Suez and proved to be a useful ground attack aircraft due to its decent payload and four 20mm guns in the nose. 28 Squadron was the last Venom unit, and it retired the type in favour of the Hunter FGA.9 in July 1962.

D.H.112 Venom FB.1 and 4

Technical Data – D.H.112 Venom FB.1	
ENGINE	4,850lb de Havilland Ghost 103
WINGSPAN	41ft 8in
LENGTH	31ft 10in
HEIGHT	6ft 2in
WING AREA	279sq/ft
LOADED WEIGHT	15,400lb
MAX SPEED	597mph
INITIAL CLIMB	7,230ft/min
SERVICE CEILING	48,000ft
RANGE	1,075 miles with tip tanks
ARMAMENT	Four 20mm Hispano V cannons and eight 60lb RP.3 or two 1,000lb bombs

The second prototype Venom, VV613, was first flown on 23 July 1950. This aircraft introduced wing fences to stop wing tip stall and horizontal fins to the wing tip fuel tanks.

The first of 17 RAF squadrons to receive the Venom FB.1 (replacing the Vampire FB.5) was 11 Squadron at Wünstorf in August 1952.

A five-ship formation from 73 Squadron operating out of Habbaniyah, Iraq, in the summer of 1954. WK482 was one of several FB.1s that were later transferred to the Royal New Zealand Air Force.

D.H.112 Venom NF.2, 2A and 3

Development
The night fighter version of the Venom began as a private venture with hopes, as with the Vampire NF.10, being pinned on overseas orders rather than on orders from the RAF.

Design
In a similar fashion to the evolution of the Vampire NF.10, the prototype Venom night fighter made use of the wings and tail booms from the FB.1, mounted onto a new wider and longer fuselage pod. Designated as the Venom NF.2, prototype WP227 (ex G-5-3) made its maiden flight on 22 August 1950. Just like the Vampire NF.10, the fuselage featured a longer nose to accommodate an AI-type radar, although the fuselage was made slightly wider so that the crew positions were not staggered. Despite the wider fuselage, neither the NF.2, nor its succeeding mark, would ever be fitted with ejection seats, much to the disappointment of the RAF.

However, the Venom NF.2 was considered a better aircraft than the in-service Meteor NF.11 and Vampire NF.10, and an order for 90 aircraft was placed by the RAF. This included a pre-production batch of seven aircraft, serialled WL804 to WL810, which were delivered between September and October 1952. The remainder were built in two batches (WL811–WL874 and WR779–WR808) at Chester and Hatfield between November 1952 and April 1955.

A third night fighter variant, the NF.3, sought to rectify all of the problems encountered by the NF.2 and NF.2A during their operational service. The main improvement over the earlier marks was an AI.21 radar, which was basically a Westinghouse AN/APS-57 supplied to Britain as part of the US Military Assistance Program. The NF.3 also introduced a hinged radome, rather than a sliding type, powered ailerons, redesigned rudders and a frameless canopy with a powered jettison system.

Service
The Venom NF.2 first entered RAF service in November 1953 with 23 Squadron at Coltishall, replacing the unit's Vampire NF.10s. While the Venom was an improvement over its predecessor, all was not well with the aircraft, which suffered from a wide range of technical 'snags' that resulted in flying restrictions being imposed on the night fighter. The problems were slowly ironed out, but so many modifications were needed that a sub-variant, the NF.2A, was introduced. This variant featured the same frameless canopy that was fitted to the Vampire T.11 and raked fins.

23 Squadron was destined to be the only unit to operate the original Venom NF.2, while three more squadrons were reformed with the NF.2A. These were 33 and 219 Squadrons stationed at Driffield and 253 Squadron at Waterbeach between April and October 1955.

An order for 129 Venom NF.3s was placed, all which were built at Christchurch with deliveries beginning in September 1953. However, the NF.3s (serialled WX785–WX949 and WZ315–WZ320) did not enter service until June 1955 with 141 Squadron at Coltishall, followed by, 23, 151, 125 and 89 Squadron in January 1956. The NF.2A remained in service until September 1957 when 253 Squadron was disbanded and, like the Vampire NF.10 before it, the service life of the Venom night fighters was short. All the Venom NF.3s were withdrawn in 1957, the last of them by 89 Squadron in November at Stradishall, making way for the next generation of jets, the Gloster Javelin.

Technical Data – D.H.112 Venom F.3

ENGINE	4,950lb de Havilland Ghost 104
WINGSPAN	42ft 10in
LENGTH	35ft 8in
HEIGHT	7ft 2in
WING AREA	279sq/ft
EMPTY WEIGHT	11,300lb
LOADED WEIGHT	15,480lb
MAX SPEED	595mph
INITIAL CLIMB	6,450ft/min
SERVICE CEILING	45,000ft
RANGE	1,000 miles
ARMAMENT	Four 20mm Hispano V cannons

141 Squadron was established as one of the RAF's premier night fighter squadrons during World War Two, and this continued when the unit was reformed at Wittering in June 1946 with the Mosquito NF.36. The Venom NF.3 joined the squadron in June 1955 and, after briefly serving alongside the Meteor NF.11, was replaced by the Javelin FAW.4 in February 1957.

The fourth production Venom NF.2, WL808, only served with the A&AEE and de Havilland, the latter for Ghost development work until January 1959.

D.H.112 Sea Venom

Development
In early 1948, at the very beginning of the DH.112 programme, de Havilland carried out a study on carrier-based variants of the Venom. The study took a more serious turn when Admiralty specification N.107 was issued, calling for a Sea Hornet NF.21 replacement. At the same time, the Venom was being considered for a career at sea.

Design
In the meantime, the prototype Venom NF.2, WP227, was being used to carry out deck-landing trials, although these were only 'touch-and-goes' as no arrestor hook was fitted to this aircraft. The trial went well enough for de Havilland to proceed with a navalised prototype NF.2, which it designated as the Sea Venom NF.20. WK376 made its maiden flight on 19 April 1951.

From the 100th production FAW.21 onwards, the Sea Venom was finally installed with a pair of Martin-Baker Mk 4A ejection seats. An additional safety feature was a rapid-inflation seat pack, which gave added thrust should the two crew have to evacuate under water.

The later version of the FAW.21 had turned the Sea Venom into a good aircraft but there was still room for a final tweak or two, which would make the FAW.22 the best of the breed. Ejection seats were fitted as standard, while power was increased thanks to a 5,150lb Ghost Mk 105 and the radar was upgraded to an AI Mk 22.

Service
The FAW.20 entered operational service with 890 Squadron at Yeovilton on 20 March 1954. The FAW.20s saw out their days with 700 Squadron, and the last examples were retired in 1959.

Although the FAW.20 featured a better visibility canopy and improved tail, the aircraft was fitted with manual ailerons, which made the Sea Venom a sluggish performer, especially in the roll. The next variant, the Sea Venom FAW.21, would have improved handling thanks to power boosted rudders and ailerons. The FAW.21 also featured a Westinghouse AI Mk 21 radar, Maxaret non-skid brakes and a Ghost Mk 104 engine.

The first unit to receive the Sea Venom FAW.21 was 809 Squadron, which was reformed at Yeovilton on 7 May 1956. The FAW.53 first saw service from June 1955 with 724 (RAN) Squadron, a pilot conversion unit, based at Nowra, until they were withdrawn in 1973, in favour of the MB.326H. Operationally, the FAW.53 served with 805, 808 and 816 (RAN) Squadrons from February 1956 until August 1967, making way for the A-4 Skyhawk and the S-2 Tracker.

894 Squadron was the first unit to receive the Sea Venom FAW.22 after reforming at Merryfield on 14 January 1957. The last Sea Venoms were the ECM variants. Seven FAW.21s were converted to ECM.21 standard, while several FAW.22s became ECM.22s. Stripped of their 20mm cannon armament, the room created was filled with a variety of ECM-type equipment and the first examples joined 751 Squadron at Watton in June 1957. Originally formed as a Radio Warfare Unit, 751 Squadron was restyled as an Electronic Warfare Unit and raised to first-line operational status on 1 May 1958 to become 831 Squadron. The ECM.21 continued to serve until October 1964, while the ECM.22, which arrived in April 1960, was not retired until May 1966.

D.H.112 Sea Venom

Technical Data – D.H.112 Sea Venom	
ENGINE	5,300lb de Havilland Ghost 105 turbojet
WINGSPAN	42ft 10in
LENGTH	36ft 7in
HEIGHT	8ft 6¼in
WING AREA	279.8sq/ft
MAX TAKE-OFF WEIGHT	15,800lb
MAX SPEED	575mph at sea level
INITIAL CLIMB	5,750ft/min
CEILING	39,500ft
ARMAMENT	Four 20mm Hispano Mk V cannon; eight 60lb RP-3 rocket projectiles; two 1,000lb bombs

Right: De Havilland Sea Venom FAW.21 XG612 during Ghost 104/105 engine, catapult and arrestor gear trials in February 1956. The aircraft was also later used for Blue Jay/Firestreak trials before serving with 700 Squadron at Ford.

Below: The third prototype Sea Venom NF.20, WK385, demonstrating the hydraulically folding wings at Christchurch in January 1953.

D.H.113 Vampire NF.10

Development
The first of the two-seater variants of the Vampire was not a trainer, as might be expected, but a night fighter, which had been modified from the original aircraft to such a degree that it was re-designated as the DH.113. The aircraft was still undoubtedly a Vampire because the wings and twin-boom layout from the FB.5 were retained but a completely new, longer fuselage pod was needed for the nocturnal role.

Design
The fuselage was much wider than a standard Vampire because it had to accommodate two crew in a slightly staggered side-by-side configuration, just like a Mosquito. Even with a widened cockpit, the seats were a snug fit and there was still not enough room to accommodate ejection seats, so the only escape was to jettison the single piece canopy. The pilot sat on the left and navigator/radio operator on right, the latter controlling and monitoring an AI Mk X radar, which was mounted in a bulbous lengthened nose that could be removed for access. The standard 20mm Hispano Mk V was retained in its original position and power was provided by a Goblin 3 engine.

Two prototypes were constructed from company funds, as the aircraft was not intended for RAF service because de Havilland was fully aware that the Meteor was already securing the night fighter role. The first prototype, G-5-2, carried out its maiden flight from Hatfield on 28 August 1949, in the hands of Geoffrey Pike; the aircraft having already been christened *Pike's Pig*. Only nine days later, Pike demonstrated the DH.113 at Farnborough, where a great deal of overseas interest was shown in the aircraft. Egypt was so impressed that it placed an order there and then for 12 DH.113s. However, tensions in the Middle East were on the rise again, and the order was embargoed by the British government, leaving the night fighters surplus. Rather than leaving de Havilland in the lurch, the order was taken over by the RAF, which re-designated the aircraft as the Vampire NF.10. These aircraft would complement the Meteor NF.11, speeding up the conversion to jets for the Mosquito crews and bridging the gap until the next generation of Meteor and Venom night fighters entered service.

Service
The Vampire NF.10 entered RAF service with 25 Squadron at West Malling in July 1952, making it the world's first jet night fighter squadron. 23 Squadron at Coltishall followed in September and then with 151 Squadron, which reformed at Leuchars in February 1952. The NF.10's service was predictably short and came to an end in February 1954 when 25 Squadron re-equipped with the Meteor NF.12 and NF.14.

There were 78 Vampire NF.10s built and, once the type was withdrawn from the night fighter role, 36 of them were converted to NF(T).10s for navigation training. Modifications included removing radar from the nose, which was replaced with concrete ballast and upgraded navigation equipment. The type served with 1 Air Navigation School (ANS) at Topcliffe and 2 ANS at Thorney Island until 1959.

Technical Data – DH.113 Vampire NF.10	
ENGINE	3,350lb Goblin 3
WINGSPAN	38ft
LENGTH	34ft 7in
HEIGHT	6ft 7in
WING AREA	262sq/ft
WEIGHT	6,984lb
ALL-UP WEIGHT	11,350lb
MAX SPEED	538mph
CEILING	40,000ft
RANGE	1,220 miles
ARMAMENT	Four 20mm Hispano cannons

The first production Vampire NF.10, WP232, was delivered to the A&AEE in March 1951. The aircraft served 1 Air Navigation School and the Central Navigation and Control School until it was SOC in late 1959.

D.H.115 Vampire T.11

Development
Prior to the arrival of a trainer variant of the Vampire, all RAF pilots concluded their advanced training and eventual 'wing' qualification on the piston-engine Harvard. As such, the fledgling pilot had no jet experience until he was posted to an AFS and operated the tandem seat Meteor T.7. With the arrival of the Vampire T.11, this situation was improved and, from 1953 onwards, the AFSs were closed down and pilots began to leave the FTS with jet experience that prepared them well for the final stage of their training at an OCU.

Design
Design of the Vampire T.11 began in the spring of 1950 under the de Havilland designation DH.115, its construction would be the sole responsibility of Airspeed and the de Havilland factory at Chester. The prototype, G-5-7 (later WW456), was first flown by John Wilson out of Christchurch on 15 November 1950. After a lengthy evaluation by the RAF, the Vampire T.11 was accepted to complement the Meteor T.7, which was already in service.

Based heavily on the Vampire NF.10, the T.11 featured a redesigned cockpit with the seats aligned side-by-side rather than staggered like the night fighters. The bulbous nose was retained for the aircraft's systems, which were accessed by a hinged bonnet-type panel. Fitted with dual controls, the T.11 was fitted with four 20mm cannons as per the operational single-seaters, and it had the capability to carry external stores. From the 144th aircraft off the production line, a one-piece canopy dramatically improved visibility and the fitment of a pair of Martin-Baker Mk 3B ejection seats must have given renewed confidence to all who flew in the T.11. The aircraft's general handling was also improved with redesigned fins.

Service
The Vampire T.11 entered service with 206 AFS at Valley, a unit detached from Oakington and 209 AFS at Weston Zoyland. The T.11 joined 5 FTS at Oakington in 1954 and the first course on the type began in May. Oakington was the first RAF station to introduce the later stage of flying training where students graduated on the Provost at Ternhill and continued on to the T.11. The 5 FTS T.11 syllabus involved 110 hours of training made up of dual instruction, aerobatics, instrument flying, navigation exercises, night flying and formation flying.

The RAF College at Cranwell received its first T.11s in 1956 to replace the Balliol. They would be the first jets to serve with the unit. The type also served with 4 FTS at Worksop, 7 FTS at Valley and 8 FTS at Swinderby. In January 1958, 7 FTS was soaked up by 1 FTS at Linton-on-Ouse to form the RAF's first combined basic and advanced flying training school. The introduction of the Folland Gnat in 1959 saw a gradual withdrawal of the T.11 from FTSs but several lingered on with 3 FTS at Leeming until 1967. On 29 November 1967, four T.11s carried out the last operational sortie, rounded off by an impressive aerobatic display before landing at Leeming.

A few T.11s remained in service with the Air Traffic School at Shawbury until 1969, leaving the CFS at Little Rissington as the last bastion for the type. From 1972, the CFS formed a new aerobatic team flown by pilots from the unit's examining wing, named the Vintage Pair. T.11 XH304 teamed up with a Meteor T.7 until 1986 when both were lost in a public, mid-air collision at Mildenhall. The loss of XH304 brought the long career of the Vampire T.11 in RAF service to a sad conclusion.

Technical Data – DH.115 Vampire T.11

ENGINE	3,350lb Goblin 3
WINGSPAN	38ft
LENGTH	34ft 7in
HEIGHT	6ft 7in
WING AREA	262sq/ft
WEIGHT	7,380lb
ALL-UP WEIGHT	11,150lb
MAX SPEED	538mph
CEILING	40,000ft
RANGE	840 miles
ARMAMENT	Four 20mm Hispano cannons

Introduced to the RAF in 1952, the Vampire T.11 became the first jet aircraft on which pilots qualified for their wings. More than 3,000 pilots gained their wings flying the T.11, which remained in RAF service until 1967. This early, heavy cockpit framed example, WZ551, is pictured in service with 229 OCU. It remained in service with a variety of subsequent units until 1964.

D.H.114 Heron and Sea Heron

Development
Basically a scaled up version of the Dove, the D.H.114 Heron was kept as 'user-friendly' as possible, the early variants even having a fixed undercarriage to reduce maintenance costs. By the time the type had reached the military, it was more powerful and more complex, yet it still retained the ethos of reliable economical operation, which had been set by de Havilland in the days of the D.H.86B.

Service
The first Heron to appear in RAF markings was the sole C Mk 2, serialled XG603, which was delivered in September 1954. The aircraft was allocated to the British Joint Services Mission in Washington for the personal use of the British Ambassador. Flown across the Atlantic on the northern route, the Heron was the first of its kind to operate in the US and remained in this role until it was sold in October 1968.

The next example was Heron CC Mk 3 XH375, which was delivered to the Queen's Flight at Benson in May 1955. Flown extensively by Prince Philip, this aircraft was briefly joined by Heron 2 (ex-GAMTS), which was given the temporary serial XL961 and used for the Royal Tour of Africa during September and October 1956 before reverting back to its civilian identity. The Queen's Flight gained two more Herons in March and April 1958 in the shape of CC Mk 4s XM295 and XM296. The final Heron to be delivered to the RAF was the only C Mk 4, XR391, in June 1961. Three Herons (XG603, XH375 and XM295) were sold onto the civilian market in 1968, while XM296 transferred to RAFG CS and XR391 to the A&AEE, both later serving with 60 Squadron. XR391 was sold in January 1971, while XM296 was transferred to the Royal Navy in July 1972.

The Royal Navy took its first Sea Herons on charge when five ex-civilian, three ex-West African Airways and two ex-Jersey Airlines, were bought in 1961. Redesignated as Sea Heron C Mk 20s, the aircraft were serialled XR441 to XR445, all of which went onto serve with a variety of units but were mainly operated by 781 Squadron. By the 1980s, five aircraft (XR444 was ditched in the Irish sea in 1972) were operated by the Heron Flight at Yeovilton until it was disbanded in 1989.

Production
The RAF operated six examples of Heron between 1954 and 1972 comprising one C Mk 2 (XG603); one CC Mk 3 (XH375); one Heron 2 (XL961); one C Mk 4 (XR391); and two CC Mk 4s (XM295 and XM296). The Royal Navy operated five Sea Heron C Mk 20s between 1961 and 1989, serialled XR441 to XR445. The Royal Navy also operated ex-RAF aircraft XM296 (June 1972 to 1989) and XR391 (on loan from 60 Squadron between September 1969 and July 1970).

Technical Data – DH.114 Heron and Sea Heron	
ENGINE	(Heron) Four 250hp de Havilland Gipsy Queen 30 Mk 2s; (Sea Heron) Four Gipsy Queen 136s
WINGSPAN	71ft 6in
LENGTH	48ft 6in
HEIGHT	6ft 7in
ALL-UP WEIGHT	13,500lb
MAX CRUISING SPEED	183mph at 8,000ft
INITIAL CLIMB RATE	1,140ft/min
CEILING	18,500ft
RANGE	900 miles

Right: Heron CC Mk 4 XM295 not long after it had been delivered to the Queen's Flight at RAF Benson in March 1958. The aircraft served until November 1968 when it was sold on to the civilian market and registered as CF-XOK.

Below: Ex-VR-NCF XR445 was taken on Royal Navy charge at Leavesden on 21 March 1961 and was initially assigned to NARIU at Lee-on-Solent before joining 781 Squadron. The aircraft gave good service until 18 December 1989, when it was placed into storage at Shawbury. Sadly, after being sold at Sotheby's in 1990, the aircraft ended its days dumped at Booker in 1995 and was scrapped the following year.

The Heron not only served the military of Britain but also Belgium, Ceylon, West Germany, Ghana, Iraq, Katanga, Kuwait, Malaysia, South Africa, and pictured here, Jordan.

Other books you might like:

Historic Commercial Aircraft Series, Vol. 6

Historic Military Aircraft Series, Vol. 26

Aviation Industry Series, Vol. 5

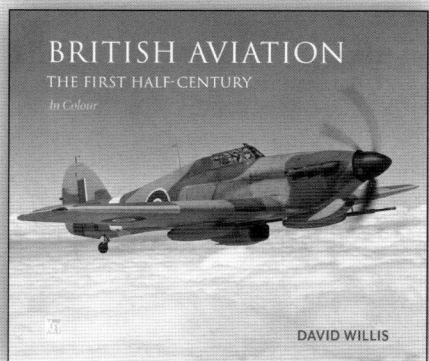

Aviation Industry Series, Vol. 4

For our full range of titles please visit:
shop.keypublishing.com/books

VIP Book Club

Sign up today and receive
TWO FREE E-BOOKS

Be the first to find out about our forthcoming book releases and receive exclusive offers.

Register now at **keypublishing.com/vip-book-club**

Our VIP Book Club is a 100% spam-free zone, and we will never share your email with anyone else. You can read our full privacy policy at: privacy.keypublishing.com